Katheryna Fedorova, from Ukraine, is an English teacher, life coach, businesswoman, photographer, writer, and poet. Before the war, she ran her English school in Kharkiv for twelve years. She is happily married and has three children. Through her spiritual and religious beliefs and her views on life philosophy, she is committed to her mission of helping others to make their lives better. She has published three books in Ukraine and one book in English, The Road from Kharkiv, a journey of pain in pursuit of love, God and sense.

I dedicate *Who Am I?* with heartfelt gratitude to my children, whose unwavering love and support have been my constant motivation. Through this book, I aim to show them that the power of dreams knows no bounds, and with determination, anything is possible.

To my loving husband, your support and belief in my craziest ideas, including writing this book, have been my rock on the journey to success.

Last but not least, I dedicate this book to myself, for having the courage to pursue the dream of changing the world and helping one billion people. I hope to realize my life mission successfully.

Katheryna Fedorova

Who Am I?

A Guide Book to Your Sense of Life

Austin Macauley Publishers™

LONDON * CAMBRIDGE * NEW YORK * SHARJAH

A CIP catalogue record for this title is available from the British Library.

ISBN 9781528986403 (Paperback)
ISBN 9781035803385 (ePub e-book)

www.austinmacauley.com

First Published 2024
Austin Macauley Publishers Ltd®
1 Canada Square
Canary Wharf
London
E14 5AA

Special thanks to my friends Tanya and Olga, who not only believed but also encouraged me to take that crucial step and sign the contract for this book. Your faith in me means the world.

To my aunt and my mom, your words of encouragement, telling me that I am smart and can achieve anything, have been a constant source of strength.

To God, my guiding light and boundless source of love, I acknowledge your presence throughout my life. Without your help, I know I could not achieve anything.

I extend my gratitude to Austin Macauley Publishers for recognizing the potential in my book and believing in its success. Your support has made my dream a reality.

Author's Note

My dear reader, I have written this book for you. I believe in you and I wish you could find out your purpose in life, realize your dreams and achieve any goals. May this book be your guiding light on the journey to discovering your purpose and finding true happiness. Your pursuit of these goals has been my inspiration and motivated me to finish the book.

I devote my book, my love, my heart to you!

Forever yours,
Katheryna Fedorova.

Table of Contents

1
'I was born!'

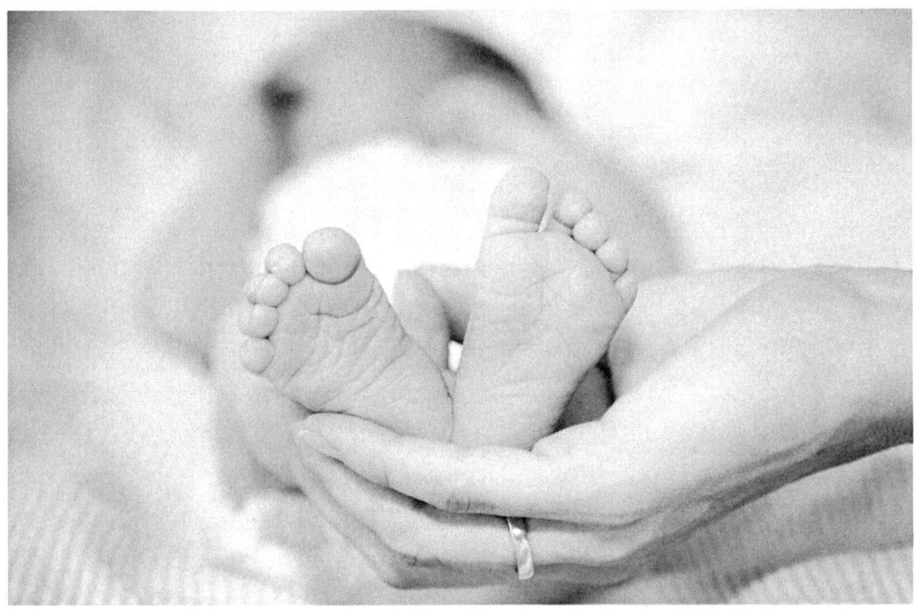

"When you have a childhood dream that still burns and tugs at your heart when you're an adult, you owe it to yourself to pursue and achieve this dream."

– Robert Cheeke

Everything starts from our birth. We are born with ready-made potentials to all our life questions. We have not opened our eyes yet, as our main basic values and emotions are imprinted in our soul. Usually our main values, which we will subsequently manifest in the world, fall into three main categories. These are the important tools and the prism through which we will act, make decisions, dream and think. They will be our main reference points in everything we do and where we go.

If you could ask yourself as a new-born 'Why am I here?', as a baby could easily answer in great detail about all the tasks that our soul packed in our life mission, all the tests that we must go through in order to obtain the necessary resources and knowledge in order to realise our purpose of life. And of course, we would answer what is our biggest value and what we can pass on to this world.

The soul of the child is still in close contact with his/her consciousness. The child can hear their soul, understands the meaning of the inner universe and feels a connection with the spiritual life that they left in order to go through the Earth life. In this map of the world, everything would seem clear and understandable. Only the child cannot speak, cannot talk about this experience and share their soul's wisdom. All his knowledge is stored deep within them. They look at the people around them through this deep emotional knowledge, through their values and their mission.

You may ask: "Why is everything so complicated? Why didn't they get the opportunity to share or save this knowledge for a longer period, so that later, as an adult, they would be able to broadcast it into the world?" The answer is obvious. I guess it would be too easy for our soul. In this case, the soul would not be able to seek, struggle, find the important answers through suffering, go through karmic trials and, of course, would not evolve. The purpose of the soul on the Earth is to become better. With each incarnation, it tries to get closer to the source of the divine light. And only in this way, through constant search and soul-searching, a person goes through all the necessary stages to improve it.

With each passing year, the world around us affects our personality. First, there are the parents whom we chose initially before our coming, then grandparents, our teachers and other participants in our evolution. Everyone without exception is a necessary element for our development. They can be loving or vice versa, they can cause us a lot of pain. But this is how we get to the truth. This is our own plan, with our own strategy for achieving meaning. It was as if we had drawn for ourselves a step-by-step plan with all the necessary difficult or successful moves. And we should not blame anyone for our hardships or pain. Our souls assumed that we would find important clues through these events and these people. Like screenwriters, we have created a personal play in which we are now living. And when our life is interrupted, and we occur in the spiritual world, we will turn on our film of life and reconsider what we actually did.

We are going through the stage of childhood, and it is the most significant part for our scenario of the future. It is exactly when our parents or teachers need to be extremely attentive to our interests, our behaviour. If their knowledge and love for us are enough to determine our predisposition to some professions, then it will be easier for us to find our way in life. Their task may even be to create conditions for our development and search for ourselves and our talents. For example, taking us to the right courses, reading the right books to us, watching movies or doing what is really important to us. If this does not happen, or worse, the parents try in every possible way to erase the picture of our values and purpose, imposing their own values and personal goals, then our process of self-knowledge will be longer and more complex.

However, there are brilliant personalities who clearly understand their tasks and what they need to do before the age of five. They are adamant in their position and it is impossible to convince them of the opposite. They know exactly who they are and why they came into life. A great example is the story of the great artist Dali. When he was less than five years old, he loved to draw. He was sure that this was his calling. And his parents tried their best to convince him of the opposite thing. Their generation of lawyers expected him to continue their legal dynasty. One day they took him to an art exhibition. Their intention was to convince their son to give up on his dream of becoming an artist. They hoped that when he saw the paintings of the great masters, he would lose faith in himself, quit drawing and take up more exact sciences. He agreed to go with them.

When they left the gallery, they were eager to ask about his impressions. They were almost certain that he would agree with them and accept the fact that he would never be like the great artists.

"Well, do you see what real art is? Do you understand that you will never be able to paint such pictures as they do?" the parents asked.

"Yes…" answered the young Dali, and his parents almost applauded at their successful operation.

"I will not draw like them, because I will draw better!" He added confidently.

Do you see how it could not be possible to break his belief by any other convictions? His soul was strong in its intention to create and give people joy and fulfilment through his work. He coped with the trials of changing his gift many more times. But, as you know, he did not betray his soul. And now, for so many years, we have recalled him as a great personality, and, of course, we have admired his work for centuries.

When we are tested for strength, we always have a choice: to agree and betray our dream, and at the same time block the flow of divine energy through our talent, or remain true to our knowledge of our gift.

It is impossible to say unequivocally that what burns within us is our destiny, but it is definitely the key to us, opening our soul. All our aspirations to do something or our childhood hobbies are always based on our search for ourselves, they are the catalysts for our realisation on Earth. They are like signals about something important about us.

To feel these signals again, you need to go back to your childhood and remember what you used to love doing and what you used to dream about.

I propose to write at least five of the most striking actions that first turn up in your memory and your childhood dreams.

<u>Actions</u>
1.
2.
3.
4.
5.

<u>Dreams</u>
1.
2.
3.
4.
5.

And now you have already touched your real self, remembered that you loved and how it filled your soul and delighted you, plunged into your thoughts and childhood dreams. How are you there? What feelings are you experiencing?

Sometimes people find it hard to recall their childhood dreams. And for some it is generally impossible to restore something in the memory of their childhood. Their consciousness seemed to have erased this information for their own psychic safety. If you have the same situation and you don't remember your childhood, don't worry too much about it. This is absolutely normal and often happens in people's lives. Despite such forgetfulness, you must become your own personal observer, persistent digger and researcher. You can look through the albums with your photos and learn more about your life, ask relatives, friends, acquaintances, even neighbours. It seems to you that it sounds strange and you will feel ridiculous asking about such things, but return again to the important task that you are pursuing and then both fear and embarrassment will be erased. This is your adventure in a story about yourself, about your talents. There it is the easiest way to reveal your talents, to find the treasure of your destiny.

There is one more technique how to find your purpose in childhood. You should buy Whatman paper, hang it on the wall. Write 'Who am I' in the centre. And you collect information about yourself by attaching stickers with those hobbies and dreams that you will collect from people from your childhood, asking them questions such as: 'Which things was I fond of? What games did I play the most? What was I good at or best at? What did I dream about? Who did I want to be in future?' Then write down the answers on paper notes, put the stickers with information about you on the Whatman paper. After that, add the answers that you will receive from your current friends, acquaintances, and your immediate environment at the moment. And the last stickers are your assumptions about yourself.

All these stickers should be of different colours: childhood, current reviews about you and your thoughts. And when the work is done, then look for stickers with repeating hobbies and/or dreams. And it is they that should lead you to thorough reflection, it is they that are subject to your in-depth analysis.

You can also practice five-minute dives into your past. Before going to bed or at another convenient time for you, remember at least one episode from your childhood. After all, memories can be hidden also because they seem irrelevant to your brain. And this is how you can extract picture after picture, then write it down in a notepad and then analyse it attentively.

You can try hypnosis and other methods, but here you need to be careful. If your consciousness hides this information from you intentionally, then it is really necessary for your soul. And the more sustainable search for yourself you are conducting, the better it is for you.

In modern society, such areas as astrology, tarot, numerology, and so on are also developing. You have the right to turn there for help in your search. But this also will not give you a full guarantee of receiving the truth in the answers you receive. For example, once a natal chart was calculated for Madonna and it turned out that there would be nothing outstanding in her life. As you can see, the prediction did not come true.

In no way am I denying the importance of any of these ways in finding yourself, but I still suggest starting with your own observations. After all, the answers often lie on the surface, you just need to scratch your memory carefully and go back as deep as possible into your history, because there you were not susceptible to the influence of external factors, there you were still close to the spiritual world and heard your soul better.

Understanding who we are and where our meaning lies is not so easy and requires perseverance and a strong desire from us to get to the bottom of the truth. Every time you open a page about yourself or even a line, your soul rejoices, as well as those who believe in you in heaven. The vital task is to find the core of our bulb. As we remove layer after layer, we expose more and more of the real us.

Practice and questions:

1. Write five activities you used to like in your childhood and five dreams from your childhood.
2. Make up a Whatman paper with all investigations about your childhood preferences and favourite things.
3. Recall the fragments of your childhood in meditation.
4. Find old albums, photos, videos from your childhood.
5. Watch the films or cartoons which you used to see in childhood, visit the places where you spent your happy time when you were young.

2
What is Your Life About?

What are your days about? What's in this?
What vital thing have you already done?
And have you managed to find major keys?
A little more and your day will be gone.
What can the hours say about you?
What do they strike about and for whom?
Can you confirm that you are always true?
Is there enough love in your soul room?
What is this moment like? And are you in?
Where is your focus and your thoughts?
This moment is the most unique you've ever been,
Begin your new life from the basic course.

Many people do not enjoy their lives or they feel that something is wrong with them, they have constant sadness and keep longing for something. But they cannot understand what exactly is torturing them. They examine their lives and are pleasantly surprised that they seem to have everything: a family, well-paid work, enough money, and their own home. But still, there is some kind of emptiness inside and they do not know how to fill this space. And then they fill this with alcohol, social networks, drugs, gambling, and so on. And further plunging into the unconscious world of these artificial 'distractors', they are losing more and more of themselves and their meaning of life. This is obviously a way to nowhere and definitely it never leads to happiness.

Why does this longing and sadness appear? It often happens because of the inability to realise the value that is inherent in us from the very beginning, at our birth. Roughly speaking, you were given gifts, they were chipped inside you and sent to this world. And you completely forgot about them, you began to live an ordinary life with human needs and requests: how to earn money, how to meet your family's needs, how to be respected in society. It is more about survival, but not about life. One day you start getting signals such as pain, illness, sadness and dissatisfaction. They try to wake you up, return you to an important mission, to the real you.

First of all, you should start by slowly waking up yourself, living more consciously, seeing the world not only from the inside, but also looking from the side at yourself and what is happening to you, analyse your life, actions, behaviour, find more and more hidden from you. Remember to that we learn best from our mistakes. You should see mistakes in your life as a positive, just learn from them.

We must be in constant self-knowledge, revealing all our special talents and abilities in order to realise ourselves as much as we can during our life. Also, we should not forget about our karmic tasks, which are of no small importance for us and our soul. Surviving on Earth is the least we can do. But is there any point in coming into this world with the goal of just surviving?

And here your years, months, days, hours are passing by. What do you fill them with? When your year is over, do you draw conclusions about what you managed to reveal about your sense and your destiny, how much you have passed on to the world of your values and talents? What about your day? How many points do you mark at the end of the day for the same achievements?

You may now begin to argue, convincing others and yourself that you work hard, that you are busy, or that this can be done later and 'now' is not the appropriate time. And when will that appropriate time come? After all, time is relative. Perceived time and real time (as per a clock) is not the same thing. You must have watched a boring film and it lasted forever and another film you enjoyed that was over so quickly. Yet they were the same length in clock time. So there is no concept of 'appropriate time'. There is a concept 'here and now'. And if you are reading this book, you are interested in your 'here and now', and you may feel emptiness that you would like to fill with your own meaning.

Can you predict for sure how long you will live? How do you know how much longer you are going to wander in this world? Our life can be interrupted at any time. Therefore, do not waste your time, your precious days, which are your bricks in building the tower of your destiny.

I suggest you treat each of your worldly days with due respect, appreciate the days, not wasting it on empty deeds or sufferings. You will have time to suffer more, and now you need to realise who you are and why you were born, absorb the wisdom of being at that moment, breathe your life and look for the ways how to hear your soul again and resume to tune it. When contact with your soul is established, when a stream from the universe passes through you, then your life will begin to be filled with happiness and joy.

In the first chapter, we explored your childhood, and now I invite you to study your daily routines. What do your days consist of?

At the end of the day today, fill out the following table:

What have you done for yourself, what insights and realisations have you got, what have you done for your dream and destiny, what have you shared with the world?	What have you done during the day? (all your usual activities of the day)

And now evaluate your day thoughtfully, how effective it was for you, your development and for the soul, which also strives for evolution and closing of those karmic tasks that it has set for itself in this life.

The day has passed, and it seems to you a daily routine, just a point that you put every day for yourself. However, your day is always a chance to change your life, make it brighter, more fulfilling, this is an opportunity where you could find something new, open the horizons of your possibilities, or stop and enjoy this day, be in meditation and silence. You are given twenty-four hours every day to do something important. Don't miss this chance. Get into the habit of doing at least one thing every day for yourself and your soul. And it won't be long before your life begins to change, and your destiny becomes closer to you.

Practice and questions:

1.   Write the list of things you have done today? Which of these things were about your soul's wishes and its development?
2.   Imagine that it is your last day on the Earth, what would you like to do? Describe it in a very detailed way.
3.   Write a little essay 'My ideal day'. What can you do today in order to achieve this dream?
4.   What do you hate doing every day? Can you eliminate some of these things from your day? If not now, when can you do that?
5.   Where would you like to be right now?

3

What Does 'Purpose of Life' Mean?

"It does not matter how long you are spending on the earth; how much money you have gathered or how much attention you have received. It is the amount of positive vibration you have radiated in life that matters."

– Amit Ray

Purpose is a very popular term in our modern age. Previously, our parents did not think so much about who they were, what their meaning of life was. They worked hard and earned money to feed their families and to meet all their needs. Although, of course, there were exceptions, those who were in a constant stream of self-discovery. In any case, this topic has now developed very quickly and it is actively discussed in different societies. There is a tendency that many children grow up and become psychologists, coaches, gurus, educators. It is a popular trend around the world. Thousands of books have been written on this subject. If you just type the phrase 'purpose of life' into Google search, you will get more than twenty-two million links. This is the most popular query in the world right now. It definitely means that it's relevant nowadays. Everyone wants to get their existential answers as soon as possible and become happy and conscious at once.

In addition, this concept is often confused with other terms, such as a sense of life, career guidance, disclosure of talents, abilities, mission, life path, and so on. They are all similar in some way, but they are not the same. Purpose of life is a broader concept. **This is the optimal combination of unique knowledge, skills, talent, experience, aspirations of the human soul with the needs of the world regarding this combination.** All components of this concept are the necessary steps, the foundation for achieving the destination. As we uncover each of these steps, we rise higher and higher in the level of awareness.

Purpose can also be depicted as a yin-yang symbol, which means: I give you = you give me back. In other words, I share my values with the world, and they give me back money, gratitude and energy. This cycle is very important. It is the meaning of our life. We give our gift to people, it is necessary for them, and we are reciprocated. You can have talents and abilities, but never use them and become useful to the world. The task of the purpose of life is to make such an exchange. The Yin-Yang is also about balance.

If you share your values generously and not take back enough from people, you become like a desert, empty and dry. In this case, you suffer from depression and lack of energy as you give away everything from you. And vice versa, if you do not share your values and realise your purpose in life, you become like a big, overfilled balloon which can explode at any moment. And it also leads to constant stress and depression. So, realising your purpose in life is always about balancing: giving and taking back your energy. It is a law of life which we should follow to achieve a life balance and happiness.

Furthermore, there can be more than one purpose during a life, it can be changed several times. For example, I have changed my purpose twice already. First part of my life was devoted to education and teaching. I launched private language schools, developed educational systems and dreamed of creating a new clever generation which will make a difference. I really wanted to change the world through teaching and study. Suddenly, after the birth of my third baby, I changed my destination and my purpose. I studied as a coach and a psychologist, started reading a lot about the purpose of life and natural talents of people. And

I made a decision to become a writer and a coach. My purpose became giving people inspiration and consciousness.

However, it is vitally important for a person to manifest in some job his key values that were bestowed upon him at birth. The meaning of a person's life is the experience of his values, which strengthen and stimulate the active principle in a person. When the destination is realised on the basis of these values, then a person feels happiness, self-realisation and fullness. The energy in him easily circulates. At the same time, the soul also rejoices at the fact that its tasks are being completed on Earth.

Therefore, he needs to find ways to realise his values and through what, which means he can change a dozen jobs in search of the best channel for his implementation. In this case, he can change the road and do different things but the core values would always be realised on his way.

Questions and practice:

1. What things make you excited and inspired? Can you devote your life doing these things during your life?
2. Do you have a fair balance between giving people your energy and getting back?
3. What is your purpose in life? Why were you born?
4. Imagine you are on the peak of the mountain, you have already finished your life road and now you are looking around. What are you like now and what vital and essential things you have done? What mission have you completed?
5. You are given five minutes on the world famous show and you should say something very important to the world which will definitely influence millions of people. Practice this speech now looking at the mirror. After that it is better to write the text down.

4

How Do You Define Your Core Values?

"The value of life can be measured by how many times your soul has been deeply stirred."

– Soichiro Honda

You need to examine your actions, thoughts and dreams. What daily decisions do you make and why? Waking up in the morning, you do a lot of things and unconsciously they all pass through the prism of your values. For example, I cook breakfast. Why am I making breakfast? Because I want to take care of my family. Family is my value. This is a simple example for defining values. This is already the beginning of your search for yourself, a deep dive into why you take certain actions and make certain decisions. You and I may love to read books, but if we go to the bookstore now, we will choose different books, because we will look for books depending on the values that we have.

In my experience of coaching, I have noticed that no one has the same set of values. All people are so individual and their decisions are unique. And that means everyone has different goals. This is also the idea of life on Earth. All people perform their specific tasks on the basis of their innate abilities, and in doing so they convey their message to the world, which no one else can repeat. Just imagine what kind of responsibility it turns out to be. Only WE have the key to certain doors, only WE have the resources that can help the world, only WE are expected to express certain manifestations of our destiny. People should always remember this. We are the conductors of the heavenly message, we are those important building blocks needed for universal well-being and peace.

Your values are within you and your task is to discover them in yourself. The list of values is rather big, usually more than three hundred of the most common ones.

Life Values

Accountability	Efficiency	Honor	Restraint
Accomplishment	Empathy	Humility	Respect
Authenticity	Enjoyment	Independence	Resourcefulness
Acheivement	Enthusiasm	Ideals	Resilience
Adventure	Ethics	Ingenuity	Satisfaction
Affection	Equality	Insight	Security
Beauty	Exploration	Intellect	Self-actualization
Belonging	Fairness	Intuition	Selflessness
Balance	Faith	Joy	Service
Career	Family	Justice	Serenity
Caring	Fidelity	Leadership	Stability
Consciousness	Fitness	Love	Spontaneity
Community	Focus	Loyalty	Strength
Compassion	Freedom	Mastery	Teamwork
Connection	Fun	Merit	Truth
Challenge	Generosiy	Money	Temperance
Commitment	Goals	Nature	Thankfulness
Consistency	Goodness	Openness	Thoughtfulness
Communication	Growth	Order	Tolerance
Creativity	Hard work	Optimism	Tradition
Competition	Health	Opportunity	Trust
Dependability	Helping others	Purpose	Understanding
Determination	Honesty	Preparation	Uniqueness
Discipline	Hope	Prudence	Vision
Diversity	Healing	Reliability	Vitality

Most often, it is difficult or almost impossible for someone to find their own set of basic values, especially when they began to search in adulthood. To do this, a psychologist or coach helps, who, with leading questions according to a special algorithm and with certain techniques and exercises, reveals the most important grains in you. If you are not a coach, then it is still worth contacting the world as much as possible, since it is through contact with it that you get to know yourself. You can't stay alone cooped up and discover your core values without being in contact with other people. You need to go out into the world and communicate, love, make friends and even get into a conflict. In interactions with the outside world, each time we experience new insights, we find grains of knowledge and wisdom. It looks like learning to swim. You can swim only if you jump into the water. The same situation with your answers. You will discover your values just if you jump into the ocean of interactions and relationships. Mingling in society provokes you to express your main features and show who you are.

People are different. And in contact with them, we take their energy, share our own, come into contact with different values. You can talk about the same thing, but it will mean one thing to you, and completely different to another person. And in this way, you can see this conflict and feel what is important for you. For example, two women are arguing in a store while buying a dress. One says that beauty is important, so that it is better to buy something bright and conspicuous. And the other does not understand at all how you can buy such a thing if it is not practical and convenient at all. For one, beauty and brightness are important, and for the other one, convenience and practicality are vital. The example is approximate, since other factors, such as confidence and the presence of fear, can also influence their choice. However, it clearly shows how people view the world on the basis of the guidelines that are embedded in the program of their basic values. The coach at this point would ask a few more questions to

understand the depth of their choice, what guides women when choosing a thing, why it is so important to them, what lies in the very depths of their subconscious and in which spheres they also exhibit such values as beauty or practicality. And thus, they would help to get to the bottom of the truth. As you can see, everything is inside you, all the answers are right in front of your nose, you just need to stop and start analysing everything that you do and why you do it.

Let's go through a simple value-setting exercise.

Look at the picture.

What thoughts do you have? Did you have a bike as a child? What did you like about cycling? What were you like and what did you experience when you owned or rode a bike? Usually, answering these questions can reveal those values that were already refracted about your thoughts and emotions at that moment in your life. In the first chapter, you wrote down your actions and your childhood dreams. You now need to continue this exercise, trying to answer for yourself the questions why you liked it and why you dreamed about it. I recommend even extending this chain of reasoning by asking the question 'Why'.

For clarity, here is an example on which you can work out all your actions and dreams for your values.

List of your activities.	Why did you like it?	your answer…why was it so valuable to you?	Why is it so important to you (previous answer)?	So what is your value?
I loved teaching dolls.	I liked sharing knowledge.	Sharing knowledge, I felt like a teacher, a mentor.	It seemed to me that the students were inspired by learning something, they wanted to become better.	Inspiration
List of your dreams. I dreamed of writing a book.	I wanted to share my knowledge and experience.	I like to be useful to people, I want to help them find their real self.	It is important for me to help them and be useful, because then I fulfil the role of a guru for	Service

			them, I realise service to them through the word.	
List of your dreams. I dreamed of writing a book.	I wanted to share my knowledge and experience.	I like to be useful to people, I want to help them find their real self.	It is important for me to help them and be useful, because then I fulfil the role of a guru for them, I realise service to them through the word.	List of your dreams. I dreamed of writing a book.

Write down all your actions and dreams and analyse. See what values you repeat, what words sound most often. They are most likely the values you are looking for.

If it's still difficult for you to work them out yourself, I still recommend contacting specialists who, in one session, will be able to analyse all your requests and find values.

Knowing our basic values are so crucial in search of our purpose of life. It is like a fundament of our sense. If you manage to understand which core values you have, you will be able to live consciously and be aware of your main mission. You can see your strength and your natural talent, something that is the most important in you.

Questions and practice:

1. Do the research about your main values using the technique given in the chapter.
2. Ask some of your friends what is your main value.
3. Write a short text about your values you've received. For example, my value 'inspiration'. Why is inspiration so important for me? When and where do I get or give my inspiration? What is inspiration like for me?

5

Live Consciously

**"From birth to death you go on living, groping in darkness with no light –
and you could have created the light. You cannot find it in the scriptures;
nobody can hand it to you. It is not purchased or sold; it is non-transferable.
But you can create it – you can put all your energies together. You can start
living consciously from this very moment."**

– Rajneesh

When you determine your main trump cards, when you find out what drives you
in making decisions and aspirations, then your life will be filled with more and
more awareness. You seem to wake up and begin to notice more meaningfully
what you are doing in the world and what is really happening in your life.

Perhaps you have been realising your values and your purpose for a long
time, or you are very close. We often evaluate ourselves but not objectively. We

think that we are at a certain stage of our journey, but in fact, we are already on a completely different line of life. It is important to define your starting point, to be aware of exactly who you are now and what you have at the moment. And now I'm not talking about financial success and social significance, it's more about your development as a person and what has already been done for the soul, what abilities you have already realised and what you have achieved in your field of destiny. You need to review what you have already done.

Evaluate the road you have travelled on, not just the desired destination. Evaluate what you have learnt on this journey.

You might shrug your shoulders and say that you haven't done anything significant in your life. But you will have realised your values dozens of times when you were in contact with people, when you overcame certain trials in your life, when you raised children, and even when you shared your successes on social networks, inspiring others.

To develop awareness in yourself, you need to learn to observe yourself and your life from the outside. Study any action or even your thoughts not only as a performer, but also as an observer. One day, after reading Viktor Frankl's book *Man's Search for Meaning*, I began to practice this kind of observation of everything that happens to me from the outside. It's like being in a movie theatre, eating popcorn and watching the fascinating drama of your life. You are the main character. And the more you watch your own scenes and listen to the characters of this movie, the more you want to change something in the performance of your role.

Often the following thoughts arise: *Well, how could I react like that, What a stupid and emotional answer, What a childish decision,* and so on. And when you completely stop liking your cinema, when it becomes unbearable to see your mistakes and weaknesses, then there is a rebellion and a desire to change your life.

However, you should not blame yourself for some wrong decisions either, because there are none.

NO WRONG DECISIONS!

Our souls created not just such a scenario of life for us, all our actions and seemingly immature decisions were provided for by it. Our other events and meetings flowed logically from them. Everything happened according to the plan, according to the clearly described line of the developing plot. And your decisions and events, which seem to you not entirely correct and sometimes absurd, were made in accordance with the level of maturity of your personality, the evolution of the soul and karmic tasks. Therefore, when watching your life in your cinema, do not throw tomatoes on the stage if you do not like what you see at all. You cannot change the past, your job is to change the present.

After watching a movie, it is better to sit down calmly and start analysing each painful scene for you. In any of your life trials, there is always more good for you than bad. Realise that pain and difficult experience are always packed with clues for you to become more aware and understand many of your questions. In addition, there are always keys to improve your life, and of course, to open new doors on the way to your destiny.

So, how to deal with each challenge and test? If someone hurt you, offended you, betrayed you, or other difficult circumstances were committed, do not try to go through them too quickly so as not to feel pain and suffering or forget forever. This is a chance for you to explore your depth, to understand the origins of this event. And suddenly it is very important for your transformation and it could obviously connect with your destiny.

Often in a difficult situation, you can go down into the depths of your subconscious and unearth the reasons that underlie it. You may be surprised, but such situations happen to test yourself and convey you appropriate knowledge. For example, before this event, you asked God to give you some qualities, such as strength, endurance, leadership, the ability to love and forgive, and so on. And so he wanted to help you and sent a certain trial to acquire your skill. Or you asked for new realisations, insights, wisdom, new paths in life. And again the sky sends you 'kind' greetings, so that you know all these truths. **Every request we make is always followed by an answer.** We are really loved, therefore, without unpacking your troubles and sorrows, you miss receiving your gifts, which you have been dreaming about for so long.

Don't you think that if you ask in prayers to become stronger and more confident, the sky will send you a box with strength and tie it with a red bow. All our desires for change are always through pain and fears. But after answering the question 'what for', a person is filled with energy and gratitude, he wants to move on.

For many years now, I have been practicing the following technique, it is called 'BUT'. Take your painful situation and fill in such a table. For example, I will share with you my situation from childhood. Once, when I was a teenager, my grandmother said that God did not give me intelligence and talents, but gave me diligence. Then I burst into tears and thought that something was wrong with me. But later, I came back to this situation again and decomposed it into good and bad. I wanted to fully understand what was hidden behind it and what it really gave me.

Offensive words "YOU HAVE NOT BEEN GIVEN GOOD BRAINS."

Minuses	But
I was sad and depressed. I had many years of self-doubt. I turned down many job offers, being afraid that they would notice my stupidity. I always prepared for lessons until late at night.	I became incredibly hardworking. If I wanted something, I always set deadlines and with work and tough discipline I always achieved my goals. I graduated from high school with a medal and two universities with excellent grades. I have always been the first and successful to overcome this fear of being stupid. Not having received strong support and self-confidence from people, I turned on my self-confidence, self-support. Thanks to the phrase 'no brains', I have become an educated woman. Thanks to my hard work, I created a business, learned several languages and mastered psychology and coaching. The ability to discipline myself helped me to write several books in different languages, courses, and trainings. I became stronger and relied only on myself. I inspired a lot of people to change their lives and achieve their goals.

There are so many more advantages from this painful situation. Surprisingly, we usually become such people who we are now just thanks to offensive words in childhood. Now imagine that if in my childhood my grandmother would not have told me those offensive words, I could not be the person I am now. They were just the necessary pushes for my changes. She realised her mission for me, actually.

It turns out again the script of the soul works. I, apparently, asked the sky to become more successful and confident. And so, through my grandmother, he pushed me to such accomplishments.

I have given an example of an analysis of an event from childhood. And if you are in pain right now, then immediately take a pen and fill in your table 'But'. Perhaps, at first you will write the pros and cons in both columns of the same amount, but then go back to the list again and add more and more 'but'. As practice shows, the column with pluses is always much larger.

Believe me, usually your most recently painful situation will be the best life-transforming event for you. You can find more pluses if you analyse during your experiences, then you can find all the reasons hidden in the depths. This is about awareness!

Questions and practice:

1. Choose one of your painful situations and write pluses and minuses of it. The task is done, when the column with plusses will be more.
2. Who has influenced you most in your life? What has changed in your personality after their impact?
3. Play a game. Close your eyes and watch your own film where you are the main character. What name would you give to your film? What is the genre? What is its idea? It would be great if you could make up the final of your film, positive final.

6
Trust and Gratitude

"What I have is enough; I am enough; I am grateful for all that is in this moment, all that is me: the chances I have been given, the things I have done, the good, the bad, and the embarrassing. I am grateful for them because they have brought me to this place. They have been my guides and my teachers."

– Paul Williams, Gratitude and Trust: Six Affirmations That Will Change Your Life

The main step on the path to awareness and your destiny is the ability to trust the world, and therefore everything that happens in your life. It is a great art to live in harmony and accept with gratitude everything that comes: both good and bad. As we discussed earlier, everything, even the most difficult circumstances of life, are somehow necessary for us and they contain essential answers and our development. And, having such knowledge, a person must completely trust the universe (God). After all, everything is sent to him or her. The main thing to know is that it is always for the good and has something important and meaningful for us, packaged deep inside the problem. And then it is not scary to live, there is no fear of making a mistake, there is no fear of getting pain or injury. Just to know that God (the Universe) is good to us and helps and guides us through difficult trials.

When something is not going well with you and it seems that everything is not going the way you planned and you think that there is only darkness and no light ahead, negative emotions fill your consciousness and it is difficult for you to distinguish the importance of what is happening with misfortune and adversity, then I suggest creating your own affirmation of trust.

My own affirmation sounds like: "I trust God and his path…"

Every time I go through some difficult test in my life or it seems to me that failures are on my way every time, I walk down the street and repeat this phrase hundreds of times. At a certain phrase, I already feel calmer, as if the light at the end of the tunnel lights up again. It dawns on me, I begin to realise the significance of what is happening for myself, I analyse what it gives me or how it protects me from something. And finally, a wave of complete confidence covers me. I see the whole picture completely; it is clear to me that this situation is an important chain of my whole meaning. Without it, I won't be able to move on to the next stage. Sometimes I even realise the connection of an awful event with my purpose and mission in life. And I want to thank God, the Universe and myself with all my heart and soul, for being able to stop my emotions and see the important thing packed inside. Gratitude emanates from me and the energy returns to me again.

Without trust, it is impossible to find yourself, your destiny, to achieve awareness. Trust is everything! Trust connects us with Divine energy, it leads us to happiness.

If you really trusted the world, you would know for sure that everything is for you, that any pain is necessary, then you would not be afraid of anything, you would be happy and always satisfied. You would soar over your life easily and simply. A person who has attained complete trust is like an enlightened sage, whose energy easily circulates and does not leak. Such people are rich in pure energy which is distributed around the world.

Do not be afraid to trust the world, do not be afraid to believe that even the most terrible event in life was created for you for some reason, and going through it with a clear awareness of its necessity is our primary task. Unless, of course, we want to find our own way and be in a state of happiness as often as possible.

Questions and practice:

1. What does 'trust' mean for you? Assess your level of trust from 1–10 (to people, to God, to Universe, to yourself). If your grade is low, answer the questions: 'Why don't you trust? What is the reason? When did it happen?'
2. How many difficult trials have you had in your life? Write a list of the most painful and vital? Do you understand the meaning of these trials now?
3. Make up your own affirmation of trust and gratitude and repeat it from time to time. Notice your feelings.
4. Remember the situations when you trusted and everything was okay. What does it mean for you?
5. Paint or draw a picture of your life when you trust. Analyse it and make a conclusion.

7
Contact with the World and Listen to the Answers!

"When the student is ready, the teacher appears. When the question is asked then the answer is heard. When we are truly ready to receive then what we need will become available."

– John Grey

Why did we appear on Earth among other different people, with different unique values, goals, qualities and purpose? The realisation of our mission always implies the exchange of energy between people and their knowledge. This necessary process of communication in the world provides us with many resources.

When a person begins the path of self-knowledge, he forgets the most important thing – that he receives the truth and his answers to his questions when he gets in contact with others. You can reveal something in yourself without contacting others, but this cannot always be done sincerely. Our answers may be subjective and may not reflect the truth about ourselves. Are you sure that you are always honest with yourself? Can you tell confidently what kind of real person you are? Most often, we either underestimate ourselves (most common cases) or overestimate when we are wishful thinking.

While contacting other people we expose our essence. We often live on a whim, not trying to understand every person who came into our lives, we do not see their message. But how many necessary keys we then do not receive, how many doors remain closed for us.

We are all the doers and guides of heaven. Through us, an important message is conveyed to someone, and at the same time, clues also come to us from other people. We are channels of communication and transmitters of information. And in order to receive an important code sent to us personally from the heavenly office, at least we need to leave our houses, talk to someone, get in touch with someone, and even come into conflict with someone.

In fact, a person reveals himself most of all when they are in a state of love or conflict. This is always accompanied by a big explosion of emotions and experience. And the more we react, the more we vibrate and the more we can get from this deep and meaningful emotional experience for us and about us.

In psychology, there is a notion called mirroring, when we see in others a manifestation of our own qualities and characteristics, but also shortcomings and dark sides. What always frightens or irritates us most in others we have also in ourselves. And, recognising in ourselves all qualities and features without exception, we express love to ourselves. And through love to ourselves, we connect with a divine energy and thank God for everything that was given us for the purpose and implementation of all our tasks. Accepting in ourselves all the flaws, shortcomings, and all the seemingly harmful components of our personality is one of the first and most significant steps towards us and our souls.

And, when you contact the world: take offense, get angry, react negatively to something that will hurt or oppress you, first answer honestly to yourself, if you have the same in you too. And when you find it in yourself, then thank the person or situation who gave you this knowledge and yourself, as you managed to realise and accept this in yourself.

Going in search of your own purpose, you need to clearly understand all the resources that you have, know yourself so well both inside and out, be honest with yourself and accept everything in yourself that was inherent in you as a person. Your soul knew for sure when it endowed you with all the qualities that you now possess. Moreover, if you cannot use and accept them in this life, if you do not pass those karmic tasks in your body, then the soul should come to this world again, choosing a life similar to yours and with your individual characteristics in order to fulfil the same mission.

Through contact, you can see the real you without your fake masks and fantasies about yourself.

The next important reason for the advantage of contact with the world is what you say or receive in communication with people. Have you noticed when you talk to someone, advise something or teach something, then new thoughts and ideas are born in you. It is as if a data current enters you and tries to seep into the world through your words and energy. This stream appears as a result of contact between people. When you share important words received from the stream, you receive useful information for yourself at the same time. And the same process occurs in another person. Just imagine how important it is to see the encoded meaning from communication and dialogues.

When I meet people for consultations, I always write down my insights after the meeting is over. Usually I get from five to ten points. I alone could not start this mechanism, only in contact with this particular person. I write down my received ideas after my speeches, after communicating with my husband, children, and parents. I am often amazed by the phrases that I pass on to them in response to some question. They hit my shore of awareness like a wave and refresh my consciousness. I also write down the necessary messages from the opposite side, trying to unravel the meaning for myself and my destiny.

You know the expression: 'Accidents are not accidental'.

And here, too, there is a certain planning of souls who agreed to meet at a certain stage of life in order to convey the keys of meaning to each other. You should take the point, finally, that all around people are souls rotating in the world, who, in contact with each other, share the keys to the doors of their destiny. Never refuse meetings, communication, contact, try to contact them as much as possible, be able to unpack their message and get important keys. Be generous to those who listen to you too. Tell them everything that you feel and that you would like to convey. On the wave of vibrations of our souls, we can give a lot of valuable things to people, and, surprisingly, to ourselves too. By passing on to others our deep thoughts received from the flow, we pass them on to ourselves.

And do not measure people by the human standards that are easily distinguishable upon contact: poor, stupid, uneducated, unhappy, and so on. How do you know which person will bring you your vital key, which person is your soulmate, who came to send you a message or correct your life path? And even a tramp on the street can be a source of your awareness and a carrier of important information for you. Any feeling of superiority and neglect of contact with people who seem to be inferior to you can deprive you of insights and streaming insights. What if they, like souls, are wiser and have chosen such a karmic path in this life. It is worth making contact with everyone, at least trying to hear the message next to people of different backgrounds. The answers may be in everyone and everything around you.

This is the power of contact, and one should not underestimate such an opportunity to find one's destiny. I suggest staying at a high level of awareness at all times, especially when you are communicating with someone or getting in contact emotionally.

Questions and practice:

1. Did you notice that while chatting with your friends or other people, you said something wise that was important for you too?
2. What irritates you about other people? Can you agree that the feature which irritates you is the one which you don't allow yourself and don't accept in yourself?
3. Have a talk with someone and be a watcher at the same time, analyse what you say, what you realise and what thoughts come to you. Write down the most interesting ones for you.
4. How often do you get the answers to your questions though the people? When were these situations and what did you get?
5. Write a list of people who were the ones who transferred you the most vital and wise messages which changed your life.

8

The Art of Appreciating What We Have

"When you don't come from struggle, gaining appreciation is a quality that's difficult to come by."

– Shania Twain

Often people are looking for a purpose, their meaning, and their eyes are deep with sadness and emptiness. They are convinced that now in their life there is nothing significant that could make them full and make them happy. They go to psychologists, coaches hoping to dispel the clouds of sadness and discover their happy path again.

Why don't they also focus on what they already have, what was given to them from birth and acquired throughout their life path? The misconception is the fact that, having found his purpose, a person will immediately become happy and he will have wings. Of course, it is important to know who you are and what you were born for, but being able to be content with what you already have and be happy in addition to knowing your meaning is an equally significant part of our life.

Despondency arises in a person when they begin to feel sorry for themselves and blame other people and circumstances for his unfortunate fate, finding out every year more and more reasons for sadness and depression. Have you tried to separate feelings and emotions from facts?

Is it so bad? Bad looks? Difficult childhood? Not enough money? Bad country? Is marriage not like you expected?

Okay, let's agree that everything is how it is (in your opinion). But if you put the negativity aside for a while and focus on what you really have, you will be very surprised how lucky you are in life.

If you take the whole world, including poor, undeveloped countries or the outskirts of the far North, or other places that are very remote with difficult, sometimes unbearable living conditions, and compare it with the place where you live, I think the statistics will determine your level of happiness in comparison with by the whole world at least 'medium', or maybe even 'high'.

It turns out that you are ALREADY lucky, since you were born in this country and at this time. You are most likely to have a roof over your head, money for food and the opportunities of the civilised world.

Personally, before moving to Kharkiv, I lived in a small town in the Donetsk region. There, cold water was given only for a few hours a day: in the morning until nine o'clock and in the evening until nine o'clock for a couple of hours, not to mention hot water, which was impossible to even dream of. Often there was no electricity, I remember many evenings with candles and with games of lotto or cards with the whole family. And, having moved, I enjoyed having hot water in the tap, the absence of problems with light and other charms of big cities. My happiness level went up significantly. After more than ten years, I go into the shower and thank God for the hot water, and in the evening I rejoice using the electricity. We do not always know what unbearable life on the street is, without means of food, without support, or even without water for many days. And what about the disabled, bedridden?

I live in constant gratitude for all the blessings I have. I am even glad that I can go to the toilet at home, I can watch a movie on the big screen without leaving home, and I can cook whatever I want. I can list endlessly what I can do and every time when I think about it, I feel the special value of these things in my life and great gratitude to God and the generous Universe for giving me such fortune.

I will also remember about my family, friends, favourite work and so on. The list will be long with lots of valuable and significant things.

Throughout almost my entire life I have been involved in charity work and have seen a lot: working with blind children, children with Down syndrome, the disabled, the poor, the homeless, those with cancer and other deadly diseases. And every time, going home after spending time with them, I felt the strength that I can do more than it seems, I felt happiness that I did not have to experience such suffering, too, and, of course, I valued my life at that moment and felt great gratitude for what I had. The fact that we can even look for our purpose, or even buy this book for ourselves, says that everything is not so bad, and you have something to thank heaven for.

So, considering all these factors, we cannot blame the heavens for our endless misery and lack of joy in life. We must honestly admit that the starting point of the path to our purpose is not exactly in the slums of depression and hopelessness, we have already at least risen to the level of satisfaction and gratitude for the blessings and environment that we have in our lives.

To make the road to your happiness easier and smoother, you first need to start living with full gratitude for every little goodness and every ray that shines into your soul. To be filled with this pure energy of love for God and the Universe for having already given so much and continues to give.

It is better to achieve your destination in a state of happiness and contentment with your life. Your path should become cumulative with happiness and thanksgiving. And when you finally reach the right door of your meaning, you will enter it with a pure heart, a smile on your face and an infinitely happy soul.

In my daily practice, there is such a tradition: before going to bed, list all the things for which I am grateful. For example, I mention such small things during the day as a delicious dinner, a pleasant conversation, an interesting movie or book, a friend's call, and so on. For me, this is not the norm or commonplace, these are gifts from heaven. And every day I love to unpack these gifts and thank for them with all my heart and soul.

I suggest you should start this habit too. It will be your first step towards your purpose. After all, this is a manifestation of trust and love to the world, this fills you with vital energy and it, of course, will increase the level of your happiness and positivity.

I noticed that after a few weeks of this practice, I really became happier, more aware and grateful. Your heart will be filled with more and more love and joy every day. And, therefore, your road to your destination will be sunnier and lighter. Along the way, you will leave crumbs of happiness for the rest of the people who will follow you.

Questions and practice:

1. Write a list of things (min 20) you have in your life which you are grateful for. If it is difficult for you to do, write this list in contrast with the poorest boy sleeping on the ground in the Indian poor district, for example.
2. Watch a film about poverty or disabled people, to see the contrast with what opportunities you have.
3. Read the book: *Chicken soup of soul, 101 Inspiring stories.*
4. Write a list of wonderful things which have happened today and which you are grateful for. Imagine them in your memory film.
5. Stand in front of the mirror and say: "Thank you for my face, my body, my life, my family, my city, my house, the planet, my talents and skills, my experience, my birth. I am so happy that I am like I am and my life is like it is."
6. And smile!

9

How to Choose the Road to Your Destination

"People don't take trips, trips take people."

– John Steinbeck

First of all, you must remember that there are a lot of possible roads for you, as well as the destinations. We discussed in the previous chapters that it is important to realise your basic values given at birth, but the purpose may be changed depending on your development and the evolution of your soul. It is important to trust any road, accept whatever comes your way, and be always in a state of awareness and gratitude.

There is such a parable 'Five Wise Men' about the purpose and life paths of a person.

The five wise men got lost in the forest.

The first one said: "I'll go to the left – so my intuition tells me."

The second one said: "I will go to the right – it is believed that 'right' comes from the meaning 'be right'."

The third one said: "I'll go back – we came from there, so I'll definitely get out of the forest."

The fourth one said: "I will go forward – we must move on, the forest will certainly end, and something new will open."

The fifth said: "You are all wrong. There is a better way. Wait for me."

He found the tallest tree and climbed it. While he was climbing, everyone else dispersed, each in his own direction. From above, he saw where to go in order to quickly get out of the forest. Now he could even tell in what order the other sages would reach the edge of the forest. He climbed higher and was able to see the shortest path. He realised that he was above the problem and could solve the problem best of all! He knew he did everything right. Others don't. They were stubborn, they did not listen to him. He was a true sage!

But he was wrong…

Everyone did the right thing.

The one who went to the left got into the very thicket. He had to starve and hide from wild animals. But he learned how to survive in the forest, became part of the forest and could teach it to others.

The one who went to the right met the robbers. They took everything from him and forced him to join their gang. But after a while, he gradually awakened humanity and compassion in the robbers. The repentance of some of them was so strong that after his death they became sages.

The one who went back laid a path through the forest, which soon turned into a road for everyone to enjoy the forest without risking getting lost.

The one who went forward became the discoverer. He visited places where no one had ever been and opened up wonderful new opportunities for people, amazing medicinal plants and magnificent animals.

The one who climbed the tree became an expert at finding shortcuts. Everyone who wanted to quickly solve their problems turned to him, even if this did not lead to development.

So, we all choose the right path. However, the question is how we will go one way or another, what we will receive and what we will reveal for ourselves and in ourselves. Knowing our values, our talents and the gifts we have, we must share them in any way of our destiny: generously, without fear of injury and ridicule.

When choosing your path, first ask yourself the question: "Will I be able to do what is important on it? Will I be able to give people my value?" If the answer is yes, then there is nothing to fear. Well, if, however, it will be too difficult or uninteresting for you, you can always turn it off. But before any turn, always turn on awareness, check your response in your soul. The soul is your compass; it will tell you exactly where to set your sails.

Questions and practice:

1. Let's play a game "What if something hadn't happened." Choose some situations, especially painful ones. And just imagine, if they hadn't occurred, what would you do now, where would you be now, who would you be like? What did this experience give you and how did it transfer you for a better person?
2. Which sage from the parable do you associate yourself with? Why? Which road would you choose?
3. Draw or paint your life road. Illustrate your obstacles and stones and hills of success and achievements. Don't forget to draw your destination, the finishing point of your way. Look at your road and think out what you could do now to make your life better and the road smoother. Add these details.

10
How to Realise Your Core Values and Why it Matters

"I understand now that my soul is my power, not perfection or my ego. I continue to teach this to my children, despite their glamorous careers. If we can maintain our core values, the exteriors take second place and become a gift, a source of gratitude."

– Yolanda Hadid

When you understand what was instilled in you from birth, what values you must pass on to the world, then your life has a certain significance. You are not just an ordinary person on Earth, you are like a missionary who came to give love, acceptance, or joy, inspiration, and so on. Why is it so important? In the first chapter, I emphasised that none of my clients in a coaching session had the same set of values.

Everyone is unique and valuable. Only YOU have been granted something special that people need to get from you, only YOU have these particular talents and knowledge. Therefore, you cannot take such a mission indifferently.

When we are searching for our meaning in life, opening our soul, we expose it more and more, making a difference. And there is a certain responsibility before the soul. It is important to understand what values drive you, what is transmitted through you.

There are two types of values:

- Instrumental (strategy)

  These values are the tools, which help to achieve goals, with the help of which a person achieves a state of happiness. These values are associated with the way of action and the realisation of goals. They are needed for something. For example, this is confidence, pedantry, accuracy, honesty, responsibility, discipline, persistence etc.

- Terminal (states)

  These are values relating to individual existence. This is what a person lives for and in what he finds the source of his happiness (or unhappiness). A person cannot explain why they are important: SIMPLY important and that's it! An example is love, happiness, freedom, faith, joy, harmony, friendship, beauty. These values are the most crucial in our life and which are the keys to our purpose.

  We need instrumental values to achieve our destiny, and terminal values – this is who we are, the components of our nature. They are our beacons, the wells of our significance.

  I want to give you another interesting parable that illustrates the significance of our values and talents.

STARTING KIT

"Well, everything – we can let him go!"

The Creator leaned back in his chair contentedly.

"What do you say?"

"Beauty! It is true that Man is the Crown of Creation!"

"So, now we add a personality with character, a soul and it's all done!"

"And what will this personality do on the Earth?"

"Good question," the Creator smiled softly through his grey moustache, and his eyes danced with small cunning sparks, "I have one idea…"

The Creator paused, as if he was thinking whether to reveal his plans or not to the companion.

"Okay, I'll tell you. Just promise not to tell anyone!"

"Promise!" Out of impatience and curiosity, the questioner agreed to anything.

"I will give every Human a purpose of life. Having it, a man will know the true happiness of being! He will be able to serve others and be self-fulfilled. Well, and, of course, at these moments he will be closest to me, he will be able to comprehend the Essence of things and the Meaning of Life. He will feel My Presence in his life."

"Awesome! What an idea! Send a Man to Earth to do what he was created for!"

"Yes, you understood correctly, my dear friend. But there is one nuance…" And His eyes flashed again with excitement. "Getting to the Earth, the Man will not know his purpose of life."

"How so? And how will he understand it?"

"Don't worry, I'll give him a hint – a starter kit in the form of talents, abilities, interests, preferences, values; I will create the necessary conditions for detection. Then let him decide whether to go his own way or not."

"Listen, it's all good, of course, but there are so many temptations on Earth. Besides that, a man will need to take care of his house and earn a living. Suddenly, in this fuss, he will not see the hints and will not recognise the purpose?"

"Well done! Bright head! But for this you will go with him – you will prompt in every possible way and instruct on the True Path."

"– I – a – a – a – a – a – a – ah!"

"Yes."

And the Creator, pushing the Man and the Angel out of his abode with one movement, slammed the door. He no longer heard the righteous indignations of his friend, since the Man with his Guardian Angel flew towards the Earth at the speed of light.

—That's all right,—the Creator said, wiping his hands after hard work,—It's done. And, my friend – I will always be there and will help you lead the Man to his Calling. Whatever happens…

As you can see from this parable, it follows that it is important for our soul to figure out how, thanks to our values, talents, abilities, to manifest our purpose on Earth. And the heavenly forces will always help us in this mission. There will be hints, signs from everywhere, important people will come and the necessary circumstances will occur. We only have to be in a state of awareness in order to be able to receive this help.

A person in search of his meaning of life will never be alone, behind him there is always a heavenly army, ready to help at any moment. After all, having found and realised his purpose, he will give the world a bright message, and this is what the angels are waiting for, trying to guide him through life in the right direction.

So, if you want to understand your purpose in life, first of all, you should find out what values you possess, which make you happy and content. They are your lighthouse which could show your road to your sense. When you understand the basic values and instrumental values which you need to realise your mission, you will reach your life destination on Earth.

Questions and practice:

1. Why didn't God give us a possibility to know our sense of life during life? Could you speculate on this question? What life would you have, if you always knew your sense of life?
2. What are your instrumental values? What are your strong features of character which help you to achieve your goals? If you can't answer, ask your parents, relatives or friends.
3. Think about your basic values and consider how they can help you to reveal your sense. For example, love is important for you, so how can you give love to the world? If knowledge is vital, how can you share your knowledge?
4. Let's play a game called 'Creator'. How would you create a man? What would you make up to realise his life mission?

11
Where Do Dreams Come From and Why?

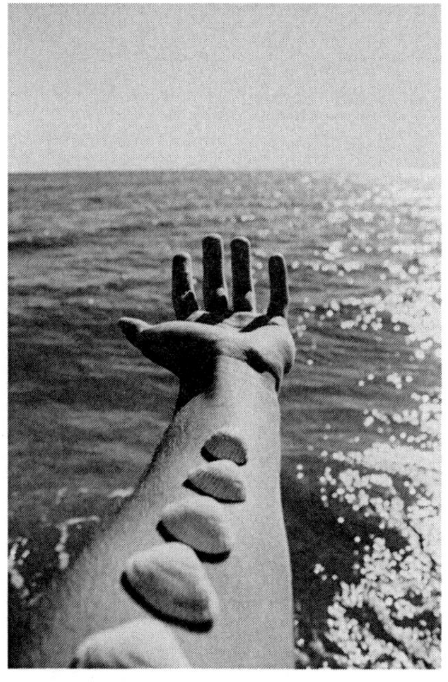

"Give your dreams wings of belief, the sky will appear within your reach."
– Bhawna Gautan

I want to start this section with a poem about dreams and their purpose.

THE PROCESS of DREAMS

Work is in full swing in the office of heaven,
A flood of requests from people arrives.
Someone gets Love, and someone's a Lesson.
Angels should send to each person his prize.

How to give people strength, hope or power?
Someone needs courage, someone needs peace.
Some people dream of happiness shower.
There's a man who is dying from griefs.
All these requests are accepted by Major.
And they go straight to the Office of Dreams,
There each angel receives his Affair.
Thinking of how to meet somebody's needs.
Suddenly he finds a man who's required,
And who is able to reach someone's heart.
The dream is sent into his mind.
Which plays a main role in the rescue part.
It is extending in soulroom deeply,
And every day it longs for reveal.
And the man feels passion distinctly
He wishes to realise inner will.
The sky is waiting for his daring actions
Gifting him strength, inspiration to go.
At last the man overcomes hesitations
his Purpose ship is starting to flow.
His dream is on, the people get sky help,
The Angel's work is successfully done.
It is the way the sky's so supportive.
It always listens to every night cry.
This is the process how dream's reaching people,
We are the messengers of Major's word.
We are the partners of holy magician,
Our sweet dreams are helping the world.

With the poem, I wanted to convey the great idea of the Creator associated with dreams. After all, dreams are the brightest signals of WHAT we should do in this world.

I am convinced that dreams come to us from outside, and in particular they come in a stream from God (the Universe). We are chosen from a billion people on Earth for a specific mission, which we realise through our dreams, ideas, projects, and so on. Dreams are like tools to help us and through us.

When you are given a basic set of values at birth, then throughout your life you must find ways to implement them in the world. So, how can you do something important for the world but not through your dreams? How can you realise your values, your energy, yourself? Dreams are a message, clues for you to reveal your worth. This is the door that you will open and touch your meaning and you will feel happy and energised.

It is important to make a decision to act and not to wait for a special opportunity to implement your ideas that have already settled in your heart. You should launch them into the world as soon as possible. Heaven also wants this, knowing that in this way it can help people on Earth through you. And, of course, it is necessary for those who you will certainly touch when you go towards your dream.

Everything in the world is conceived in an interesting way: each person can get sky's help only by contact with a certain person, and the message can only come through someone specific. How does it work? Now I will give an example.

Let's say you dream of becoming a psychologist and helping people achieve harmony. However, you are afraid to go into this profession, or even have already completed training, and do not dare to start the practice. So, while you are being afraid of starting, in the world dozens, hundreds, and maybe thousands of people are looking for you. They go to the most expensive psychologists, but do not get the desirable result. According to the scenario of heaven, you should definitely meet and contact. Only YOU could help them. And if you still have not realised your dream of becoming a psychologist, these people may receive something, but not in full.

The same thing happens with other dreams and professions. People are looking for their doctor, photographer, cook, writer, actor, babysitter and so on. They need only YOU, with your individual resources and talents. And your disbelief in yourself, fear and failure to realise your dream deprives a certain person of receiving a heavenly gift from you. By choosing not to do what you so desire, you take responsibility not only for yourself, but also for the recipients of your cause.

When an idea comes to you to start a business, launch a project or go into a profession, it means that heaven has chosen you, that you ALREADY have the necessary resources for this. It sees deeper and more objectively than you yourself estimate. Resources are your basic and functional values, your qualities of character, your spiritual characteristics, and they also know about your purpose of life.

Having received this dream, you must understand that you are ready to launch it into your life, that you have everything available, and most importantly, you have the support and help of heaven. It is a great honour to be chosen for such a mission. Therefore, every time when you receive such ideas, dreams, you should accept them with gratitude and know that you are unique and valuable. And you must try to take the first steps. The road will definitely appear when you start moving along it.

There is a theory that heaven waits up to three years until you realise their message in the form of a dream. If you continue to wait for the right time or circumstance further, then it transfers the dream to another person with a similar set of resources. I am sure that at least once in their life every person has noticed how someone implemented their ideas and became successful in the end, and he bit his elbows because he missed the opportunity to do the same.

The sky cannot wait long, it needs to help those who pray for it in their prayers and tears. It gives our dreams to another executor, because it is important to someone who needs it and it does not give us a lifetime to think about.

A dream is a chance to get happiness and be more valuable to people. And if people, receiving dreamy messages, jumped for joy, as if they received a gift from heaven, and immediately shared them with the world, then life on Earth would become much happier, more beautiful and more harmonious. The cycle of goodness would work much faster:

<a person asks God – he sends a dream to us – we realise the dream – the dream reaches the person asking God>.

Questions and practice:

1. Write your dreams from childhood, dreams from youth and dreams now. Min 3–5.
2. What would have people had from you, if you had realised these dreams? Or what didn't they get from you?
3. Remember the situation when you obtained some help or vital things from people and managed to cope with some difficulties in your life. What did they have to do or achieve in order to give you what they did?

For example, some doctors, psychologists, writers, actors or people from other backgrounds.

4. Let's imagine, you have already realised one of your dreams. Close your eyes and watch this film in your mind. What do you think about it? What do you feel in your body? In your soul? Write down what you have seen or you can draw a picture.

12

Where to Get Energy for Dreams?

Should you find yourself in a chronically leaking boat, energy devoted to changing vessels is likely to be more productive than energy devoted to patching leaks.

I was considering whether such a chapter in this book is needed and I came to the conclusion that it is still necessary, since we often do not achieve our goals, do not realise dreams and purpose due to lack of time. I asked people: "Do you know what you want?" Most people say they have a dream and available resources. Why don't they try out? And they often answered me that they did not have time for this, that they will start a bit later, when they are freer. And at the same time, they ask me a counter question, how do I manage to do everything, how I have so much time.

The answer is simple. I don't have a lot of time, but I have enough energy. And that's why I want to talk to you now about the management of your energy, not time. It seems to me that it is not just necessary to keep up with everything, but to have time to do something effectively. Everything must be in harmony and in balance.

For all your achievements, goals, dreams, plans, work – all these things you certainly need a certain amount of energy. When I plan my day, I am contemplating: 'on this day, I need so much energy for certain points of my plan. Where can I get this energy?'. To accumulate energy, everyone has their own sources. I advise you to prescribe yourself 5–10 sources of your energy. It is desirable that these are not some large-scale ones (go to Disneyland, etc.), but something elementary that you can receive daily and simply. There is a feeling that you have done something and you felt more power. So this activity gives you energy.

Having determined your list of energy sources, you must allocate a time and a place during the day where you can receive this energy. For example, I can take a nap for half an hour, meditate, listen to music, read, take a shower, have a bath, and take a walk in the park. I know that with this energy, I can do great things.

It seems to us that we need to work more and more, in order to accomplish a lot on the way to our dream. And I think that we can work not so much but to get much better results. I receive energy and give to achieve a balance. It is impossible to be happy and successful without such energy exchange in life. It is desirable to recharge with energy before your body and your soul demand it. For example, I know every day that if I don't build up energy, I won't be able to do certain things. And it is desirable to do all this before my body says: "I'm tired! I can't do it, as much as possible!"

Therefore, the correct cycle of obtaining and spending energy: when you pre-charge before you are used up. When you understand this thing, you will almost never get tired. If you are exhausted, it means that you have not taken energy before. Therefore, I simply do not reach insane fatigue, when I do not have time for anything, because I simply have no strength anymore. I just know that I will take the energy before that, so that later I can channel it in the right direction.

The second point is not to spend more than an hour on any activity. Of course, this does not concern events where it is impossible to do less than 2–3 hours. But if it is possible, split up your business by approximately an hour and do breaks.

I will highlight my example again. I have to work (I teach English or give consultations by appointment, they last about an hour). An hour later I rest, drink some tea, look out the window, and think about something completely different. And then I come back and go again to spend an hour. Then I rest again for 5–10 minutes.

That is my formula:

Fill the energy an hour working – to fill the energy – an hour working and etc.

If I have more than two hours, I feel like my battery starts to run low. So I always try to keep my energy level up to the green mark. And I'm always positive and very energetic.

And remember, if you are doing one thing, then do not be distracted by other things. For example, when I read a book, I read a book. It is a popular Pomodoro Method: When a person does something, he should only do it. This is very important, because it is again about energy consumption.

That is my secret: not doing a lot, but distributing my energy effectively. If I work, I just work, I don't get distracted by anything else. If I'm with my family, my phone is on silent mode. By nature, women are multitasking, they can do many things at the same time. But I realised that this is an inefficient way. It is better to do just one thing at a time. It turns out that you do it faster, more efficiently. You spend from a half an hour to an hour on it and go to the second task. There is even an app for the Pomodoro method.

A mandatory rule for me is the circle of life balance. We usually build a balance circle at the beginning of the year and check it at the end of the year. At the beginning of the year, we set where we would like to improve, improve our balance circle: family, finances, career, development, health, environment, entertainment, etc. If there is a deflection somewhere, you will not get anywhere on such a broken wheel. It will slow you down, and you still won't achieve anything. For example, a person works very hard and tries to earn a lot of money (his finances are already at the level 9), and the level of the family sector is low or he spends little time on health. And therefore, no matter how much he earns, his wheel of success will not go far. His life will constantly slow him down: either he gets sick, or something will happen in the family.

Our lives will always strive for balance – we will always stop to fix something somewhere. Therefore, I suggest doing the same for our wheels. Avoid breaking down when you have already stopped and repairing your wheel, but try to pay attention to the missing points at the beginning of the year and start working on them all year.

For each month, I prescribe what things in each area I need to improve. Then I write it weekly and even daily. Every day I think about all the quadrants of my wheel. And I do not forget to fill myself with impressions and vivid emotions, I stop myself when it is necessary for me and my body.

The more we somehow stop ourselves, fill ourselves up with energy, the more impressions we get, the more we create, generate new ideas. That's the whole secret. Not when you work hard, but when you are just passive, you are in a state of getting ideas. Inspiration flows through you only when you are in a state of harmony. If you read the books of great people (Mendeleev, Einstein, etc.), they got brilliant ideas that changed almost all of humanity, thanks to the fact that at that moment they were just doing nothing. When a person's brain is not tense with active activity, at this moment it is very easy for the sky to convey a message to us. Therefore, periods of a harmonious state give us more than when we are in a state of constant anxiety, work, striving to do everything. As a result, we are exhausted, and nothing new comes.

I live in a circle of balance and every day I check if I have gone through all the sectors. If I see that everything is fine, I go to bed. If I see that somewhere I didn't improve something in a troubled sector, the next day I focus on it.

The next important issue is the ability to divide cases into urgent and non-urgent cases. I have improved my types: urgent things that will immediately bring me income, and non-urgent things that will bring me income a bit later, but they also include my development, the realisation of my dreams, and even my purpose of life.

Having rest seems to be also a non-urgent matter but it can bring income in future. I will prove it now. When I have energy, I can reach some heights, because I accumulate my power. It is wrong to consider the rest from the position: "I'm lazy, I don't do anything."

For me, this is a storehouse of certain knowledge, certain clusters of opportunities. By giving myself time to do these non-urgent things, I know it will add up to a lot later. Therefore, I take this more seriously and do not say that I am lazy.

Reading books is also a non-urgent case but it might give us a vital impact on our life. Everything that happens in our life is for a reason. Any book, any event, any person appears in our life in response to a certain request, and certain responses come to this request. I sincerely believe that books are also these responses. If I read a book and something resonates with me there, I close my gestalt in this way, or at least find out the clues. From reading books you get motivation, confidence and optimism. Sometimes even one line at the end of a book can completely decide your life. Books contain a lot of resources for us.

I would like to stress the connection between decisions and energy. It is necessary to minimise decision making during the day. And it helps a lot to reduce your energy consumption. Elon Musk and Steve Jobs wrote and talked about this. For example, they only wore certain clothes (Steve Jobs had a black pullover). They argued that in order to achieve success, generate new ideas, and create some kind of super machines, they minimised the number of decisions made during the day. For example, they did not choose outfits for long – they put on the same pullovers, sweaters that they had in a certain place and they did not waste time on it.

Every day we make about a thousand decisions. For example, we spend at least a hundred decisions on the choice of food: drink water or not, add more sugar or less, go to this cafe or another, have dinner or not, diet or not. We spend money on this and we do not have enough energy to come up with a new project or finish something. It's simple: spend less time making decisions.

If you can save on something, save on some areas. Therefore, at home, breakfasts are scheduled by day: Monday – pancakes, Tuesday – scrambled eggs, Wednesday – porridge, etc. When I go to the store, I also know what to buy, and I don't have to spend a lot of time and energy choosing something, because I know what I'll be doing for breakfast. So I save energy for making decisions about food. I try to put off things that I will wear tomorrow. It is better to save energy as much as possible on unimportant things and put it all into the important. If we spend our lives on trifles, then we do not do some super-important things for ourselves and for the world, realising our purpose.

It is said that we can work a lot, and in the end there will be a big output, we will earn a large amount of money, we will be able to buy some things for ourselves. We are focusing on this. And once I understood that when we work a lot, we can have less exhaustion than if we, having accumulated a lot of energy, can do the same task.

Never blame yourself if you haven't completed all the points of your daily plan. You can't do this, otherwise the energy exchange is disrupted, the flow is disrupted, and as a result, the next day you will not get what you get. I always think that you should listen to yourself, but do everything by splitting your goals. There is a phrase: split up your achievements/goals, mark at each stage; 'I won here'. (I wrote one chapter, wrote the second – you have already done 30%, 40%). It doesn't matter if you've succeeded or not, it's what path you've taken that matters. And when you see that you are moving along this path, it means that some process is taking place, and you should thank yourself for this.

Obviously, when we are realising our purpose of life, we are energetic enough and happy. But sometimes on our way to the purpose, we should control our level of energy thinking about our mental and physical state.

If I am happy in what I do and see some advantages in it, then I want this sense to be transferred to someone else. I want each of you to see that everything is possible, any dream that seems completely unrealistic can be achieved. Why am I not afraid to dream? Because I know that any dream can be planned. All achievements depend on your energy. Therefore, if you feel tired, stop it and fill yourself up with energy!

Questions and practice:

1. What is your level of energy now? Assess it from 1–10.
2. Write min five your sources of energy (Easily and fast realised) and do something from the list. Do that every time when you need more energy.
3. Think about your dream or goal. Write down the possible steps to gain it. Focus on your first step. And try doing this for 30 minutes. Try out a method called Pomodoro. Don't get distracted. If you do that every day or oven once a week, you can achieve any goals.
4. Think about the things which get your energy and make you low. Can you eliminate them or reduce their influence?
5. Allow yourself to have a rest for some time and notice what ideas will come after that.

13

Helping a Person, We Create a Wave for Millions

"We think the journey of the wave ends when it reaches the shore! No, it doesn't! When the wave reaches the shore, it changes something on the shore. When something changes, a new story begins there. This story is also the story of the wave; the journey of the wave continues in another form!"

– Mehmet Murat Ildan

When you help one person, then the flow of your energy does not end with one person. The knowledge that you can pass on to one person can then move on in cycles to other people. And it is not known where your help may end. Most often, according to the karmic laws of energy, your good intention should come back to you.

The world would not be in balance and harmony if there were no helpers. They are needed. A lot relies on them. Some help may not just transfer knowledge and energy, it can become crucial in the life of a person, and possibly the whole of humanity. And I'm not joking at all, speaking in such global terms. We can shelter a tramp and feed him, and he will continue this chain of goodness further. Perhaps he will not have significant change as you expected, he will not suddenly become a decent citizen, but he can become infected with your kindness and pass this torch of goodness on. And something else will happen as a result of your meeting. And even your life can change in some way after contact with such a person. We can only guess what our help or some action in relation to any person can influence.

Once I was on a bus and saw an elderly woman. She was poorly dressed, but still did not look homeless. Her eyes were sad, she looked out the window and thought about something. When she got off the bus, I ran after her and offered to go to the store together and buy her whatever she wanted. She was so surprised and a little bit shocked that she burst into tears in surprise, but in the end she agreed to my proposal. We bought two packages of products. She left the store happily. I just wanted to show her that free goodness exists. We said goodbye to each other. Several months passed, I accidentally met this woman, she was standing near the market and handing out food from a bag to vagrants. I went on with a smile, I was so happy that she became a source of good for others. And then these vagabonds will probably do the same. This is how we do not know how we are changing not only the life of one person, but hundreds of people.

At that moment, the idea crossed my mind. We help through the people and with the help of them. And this important insight gave me the belief that the result of the good that I can bring to the world is not always as obvious as it may seem to me. We often play the role of launching a chain reaction of certain actions, events, feelings of a large number of people.

It seems to you that your life is not so significant, but you could serve as an important support for some person whose life task is to help a thousand people. It turns out that you are an equally valuable chain in this process of goodness.

It also concerns our realisation in some business. For example, you are not only a teacher who teaches a certain subject, but your task is to convey certain knowledge to a particular child, whose mission is to create something important in the world. And it turns out that the teacher plays an important role in the development of this future genius. It means that by helping one special child, you are also participating in saving millions of lives that the future genius will help in the future.

Often our meaning of life lies in contact with a certain person, helping him, conveying a certain message, perhaps simply believing in him. And all his achievements are also our merit, to some extent. Without us, there was, perhaps, no further development of his success.

I like one old joke about the meaning of life:
A person dies and goes to heaven. Apostle Peter meets him.
Person: I'm sorry to bother you, but I have one question for you.
Apostle: I hear you.
C: I have lived quite a long life, but I never understood one thing. Tell me, what was the meaning of my life?
A: Do you really need to know?
C: Yes, I do.
A: Remember, in 1973 you were traveling on the Moscow-Krasnodar train?
C: Uh…well…
A: And you also met in a compartment with fellow travellers
C: Probably…
A: And you went together to the restaurant in the train
Ch: Yes…
A: And a woman was sitting at the next table
C: Maybe…
A: And she asked you to pass the salt to her.
C: And I gave her the salt.
A: And you gave her the salt?
C: Passed.
A: Well, here it is…

This anecdote clearly indicates that the man's task was to pass the salt to this woman. One can only wonder why it was so important to her at that moment. And suddenly, this woman was an important historical figure, and then it was a very hard time for her and she wanted to do suicide. And when he gave her salt, something clicked in her head and she changed her mind. There may be a million versions, but the meaning is obvious that we are the carriers of something important and valuable every day, which can affect the entire course of history in general.

Let me give you another example from life. I hurried to my poetry performance. I was traveling on public transport and was very worried whether I could convey everything that the guests would come for.

Suddenly, next to me, a woman in her fifties turned to me: "You look very beautiful in this blue dress. You are like a princess, you really shine."

And she smiled. It was my stop to get out. I thanked her and ran out of the subway. When I walked to the building where I was supposed to perform, I already felt a surge of strength and energy, I seemed to be on fire. I was very excited and happy throughout the performance, I managed to tell and share a lot.

When the concert ended, I said: "I want to thank on my behalf and on your behalf that the sweet woman in the subway who lit me up with her words and smile. If not for her, I might not have been able to convey my knowledge to you so emotionally and energetically. It turns out she helped you too."

This is how influence wave theory works. We help one, and he helps others. You do not always know how and when your good deed can be taken and moreover, you do not know by whom and where. Your airplane of goodness can fly around the world for many more years, creating more and more chains of influence. Therefore, never doubt that your life is not as valuable as the lives of other more successful individuals.

We can realise our purpose several times a day when we share something with the people around us. Even our children, grandchildren, students, neighbours are all our channels of influence on the world. Therefore, it is worth being more generous with help, support, and a smile.

And if someone asks you to give him the salt, do it. And suddenly, this is your meaning.

Questions and practice:

1. Remember the situation when someone did something for you and influenced your life deeply. What was it?
2. How often did you inspire people? Remember about them and see what they are doing now. Maybe, you were a necessary trigger at that moment and now they can still go on further.
3. Think about your dream job and think how many people you could help and what waves you could make.
4. Watch the film: *Pay it forward.*

14
How to Realise Your Uniqueness?

"No matter what your differences are, you have to embrace them and be proud of the way you are."

– Jazz Jennings

At one of my coaching consultations, I asked the girl a question about her uniqueness, to which an ambiguous reaction followed: "Well, I don't know. Maybe I don't have it?"

The girl immediately became sad and lowered her head.

But I was able to help her regain her confidence when I began to ask coaching questions. With each question, she raised her head higher, and a smile appeared on her face. In the end, she clearly realised her uniqueness.

You must know what is valuable and unique in you. It is particularly in our uniqueness that we can discover our purpose. We are all, unequivocally, unique people with a unique soul and its tasks. We have been given that which no one else in the world has been entrusted with. We are the only bearers of our gift. And our uniqueness affects how we realise ourselves in life, what we achieve.

How to understand your uniqueness?

We need to collect answers to these three questions from the people we know:

1) What do people get when they contact me?
2) How do people feel when they contact me?
3) What do people want to do after contact with me?

This is another way to find your own peculiarity, that deep and intimate that we somehow broadcast to the world. We have already discussed that through contact with people we can find answers to our existential questions. So here's a clear formula for you, how you can know your uniqueness.

A person can try hundreds of professions in a lifetime, but he is unlikely to be able to lose the valuable gift that is inside him. He will unconsciously behave with others in a certain way, sharing himself through various channels of relationships: words, actions (deeds), emotions, reactions, and so on.

How to understand this in practice? For example, take my life experience. My first profession was a lawyer. I worked at two plants as a lawyer. Sitting in the office was very tiring for me, and when they announced a break for lunch, I ran to the dining room to chat with my colleagues there. At the table, I listened to everyone and then tried to cheer them up, to say something useful that would help them make a decision or be inspired. After working as a lawyer, I became an English teacher. I have worked with children and adults. And not a single lesson passed without telling them something inspiring, launching a mechanism of purposefulness and self-confidence in them. Even later, I wrote a book about the success of my students, revealing the topics that we were able to discuss with them in the learning process. I was not just an English teacher; I was an inspirational coach in every class. I couldn't help it. Something inside me just broke free and was broadcasting to the world. I wanted everyone to be happy and perform feats for themselves and their happiness, fight and follow their dreams. Then I started writing poetry and sharing it with people. In each verse, of course,

I again inspired, gave faith and significance to people's lives, I wanted to give them my energy and strength, to captivate them with my unbridled passion for life. After poems I turned into prose, performing on stage in the format of poetry evenings, trainings, motivational concerts, interviews, and so on. My next step was psychology. I was trained as a psychologist, which significantly changed and added me more tools to inspire people. After that there was a course on transformational games and coaching by purpose.

After each stage, my power of inspiration increased. I followed what people in contact with me constantly told me, "Katya, you are so inspiring!"

And so my formula developed: no matter what I did, I somehow inspired people. And the profession did not affect how I realised my purpose. In each of my activities along the path of development, I constantly strengthened my mastery of inspiration.

This is how your values are realised. People always feel certain vibrations when they are around you. Consciously or not, you will certainly give them what they need so much from you. If they do not have enough strength, and you are a strong enough personality, then people receive this strength from you, they give them a message to do something impossible. Or vice versa, tenderness and comfort emanate from you, and people take this warmth and softness.

I remember, many years ago, a girl with two children lived in a neighbouring apartment. She was so calm, homely, loving her children and husband. When we walked with the children in the yard, I loved to feed on her energy of feminine warmth and tenderness. As soon as I talked to her a little, I would come home and become a more caring and affectionate wife. I was her opposite, but I so wanted to add a little of this femininity and warmth to myself. And I received this resource from her, which then somehow survived and took root in me.

Thousands of people come into our lives with their special gift, which they pass on to us, touching us and our souls. And we give ours in exchange. This endless exchange of energies leads to the fact that we develop, become better and open more and more new horizons of possibilities.

There are no people who are not unique. Never think that you are mediocre or the same as everyone else. That doesn't happen. This would be contrary to human nature and divine design. We all carry a certain code; we just have to open it for ourselves by choosing the right password.

Questions and practice:

1) Conduct such a survey among ten to twenty people from your inner circle, write down their answers, find common and repetitive ones in them. It is precisely these features that will be your gifts, your uniqueness.
2) Try to write a little essay: 'What is my uniqueness? What do I have in particular that nobody has?'
3) Draw yourself as a unique and precious stone. And describe its features.

What do you get in contact with me?	How do you feel in contact with me?	What do you want to do after contact with me?
1.		
2.		
3.		
4.		
5.		
6.		
7.		
8.		
9.		
10.		

15
Freewriting – As a Method of Self-knowledge

"You can make anything by writing."

– C. S. Lewis

Freewriting is a writing technique that helps us enter a creative state and access the ideas and knowledge hidden in the depths of our soul. The range of application of this technique is very wide – this is writing texts, and overcoming creative blocks, and finding unexpected solutions to complex problems, and developing creativity, and even relieving stress.

Freewriting is the recording of a flow of words without self-censorship and stops, the task of which is to bypass the inner critic. And most importantly, this method helps us to talk with our soul.

Many years ago, I read Mark Levy's book, *Freewriting* and was inspired by the idea of freewriting: write with your soul, do not evaluate, do not analyse what is written, but simply move your hand in a state of meditation. It can be compared to playing the piano in an empty hall, not worrying about notes and sound. You just write, plunging into the waves of your subconscious and going deeper and deeper into yourself.

It was then, after reading the book, that I began the practice of freewriting. I wrote for a while: first I timed it for five minutes, then every week I increased the period of writing. My maximum was thirty minutes. But on average, I usually write no more than ten to fifteen minutes. In freewriting, it doesn't matter how long, it's important to write non-judgmentally and try to do it a little bit almost every day. Then the dialogue with your soul will be easier, there will be less internal resistance and control.

How does freewriting work? The first step is to find the time and place for it. It is desirable that no one interferes with you and nothing distracts you. Perhaps it will be early in the morning or before going to bed, ideally choose a place of your power: a forest, mountains, a field, and so on. In any case, this place should be right for you.

Instruction

1) Preparation. Take an alarm clock, a pen, and some blank sheets of paper. Set the alarm for five minutes the first time, then try to increase it to twenty.

2) Work. Write whatever comes to mind (with or without a chosen topic) until the alarm goes off.

3) Making sense. When you finish your work, take a good break and carefully read what you have written (preferably aloud – this way the text is perceived more correctly). Mark live fragments that can be saved and used in future work. If you have any ideas or questions, write them down. Take a marker and immediately highlight the thoughts and ideas that are most important to you that emerged during the freewriting process. Do not delay, but immediately write them down in your notebook or notes on your computer (phone).

Freewriting rules

- Write quickly, without stopping and rereading what you have already written until the alarm rings.
- Do not try to write in such a way that someone likes it.
- If your thoughts suddenly take a wild turn, don't tell yourself: "This is stupid, you need to stop," but keep writing.
- Do not correct mistakes, do not cross out anything, do not follow grammar and punctuation, logic and style. Your main task during freewriting is to stay in the flow.
- Write in complete sentences (not a list or a set of words).
- Be as precise as possible in the details – describe the texture, smell, sound, etc.

I recommend that before you start writing, do yoga or at least go through a short meditation session. You need to be in a state of rest and relaxation. If meditation and yoga do not work out, then at least lie down on the floor in the pose of a starfish and lie down for a few minutes without thinking about anything. Then slowly get up and write!

Freewriting should be done for several months or even a lifetime. If contact with your soul is important to you, then you should adhere to this ritual constantly.

I confess to you that often my poems were written as a result of freewriting. I sat down at the table and wrote everything that was dictated in my head. I often did not understand what the poem would be about, what its message was, but I stubbornly continued to bring it to the end. Line by line, rhyme by rhyme, I created something special and valuable. And above all, for yourself! And when I reread what I managed to write down, I realised the special importance of WHAT had just happened to me. I felt the need to quickly share this with the world. Without even waiting for the morning (usually I wrote before going to bed) and with not quite ideally recited lines, I posted the verse on the net in order to fill other people with energy from the verse that had just been transmitted to me by my soul as soon as possible.

I am also writing this book using the freewriting method. My knowledge of purpose is written in books, of course, but most of what I write is a stream that I try to translate into words and sentences that come out of me as I write.

Sometimes it was very difficult to build a clear system of presentation, the flow mixed a lot of important information into one whole, first, through freewriting, I had to pour everything onto paper and only then disassemble everything that could be transformed into a word. Without freewriting, this book would not exist, and neither would my other books. I can't imagine my life without writing, and I am grateful for freewriting, which gives me the opportunity to create value for people, fill gaps in awareness and make the world more fulfilling and happier.

Questions and practice:

1. Try out freewriting. Ask yourself any question that worries you now, mark 5–10 minutes and write without being distracted by anything. Ready?
2. Read Mark Levy's book: *Freewriting.*
3. Do meditation and listen.

16
About Passing on Our Values
to Our Children

When you have a lot of resources, the most important thing is to have had good parents and to have been brought up by people who gave one the proper values.

Once I was riding the subway and a friend of mine sat down next to me. We began to talk about raising children. She shared with me her difficult situation with her son, who did not want to be hardworking and purposeful in his studies. She reproached him for finding different and easy ways to get good grades all the time, but stubbornly did not want to study.

At that moment, a rebellion rose up inside of me. I wanted to protect the child, asking her just one question, "Why should he be as hardworking and purposeful as you are?"

But she did not take my advice, and I did not impose my opinion.

When I came home, I became more and more immersed in the topic of raising children. I asked myself if we should pass on our core values to our children. After all, he or she was born for his or her life purpose, which may not coincide with ours and, of course, other values and strategies will be required for its implementation.

After much thought that day, I came to the conclusion that we still need to give our children what we are valuable and endowed with, but do it carefully, analysing WHAT we give and whether our child will need it in future.

I came up with a value check algorithm for myself through three questions:

1. WHAT do I want to pass on to my child?
2. WHY does my child need this value or quality?
3. HOW can I convey this value or quality to him?

It is in this sequence that you need to ask these questions and listen carefully to what answers come to you.

I propose to test this theory of three questions. Again, I will take an example from my own life. I have three children: two sons and a daughter. I often thought about what I would like to leave in their memory, in their heart, in their character from me. After all, the realisation of my purpose also involves the transfer of my values to the people closest to me, and in particular to my children. And I decided that I want to give them my love for people, kindness, optimism and enterprise. Started with love.

1. What do I want to give, what to convey and what to teach? I want them to grow up as people who know how to love unconditionally, give their love to the world and help those who lack this love.
2. Why do they need it? They will be able to apply this in their future families, in friendship, and they can pass it on to their children.
3. How can I convey it? I will be an example for them: to love them, my husband, as well as all the people I will meet on the way. My children will watch me and my good deeds from the side. I have been doing

charity work for many years: I teach for free in centres for blind children, with Down Syndrome, incapacitated and cancer patients; I help children from poor families or the homeless. Sometimes children participate with me in the actions of kindness, and come with me to different centres. My son once baked cupcakes for a dying grandmother whom I wanted to help. In addition, I read books about kindness and love, sing songs and watch films on the topic of human relations and kindness.

This is how I convey my value of love to them. I do not demand to be the same as me, but simply involve them in my world of love, drawing them pictures of goodness with my actions and words. And this is their decision what to take from my stream.

However, not all of my values passed the three-question exam so successfully. For example, I would like to give my eldest son perseverance and optimism.

1. What do I want to convey? The ability to see the goal and go after it persistently with the confidence that everything will work out.
2. Why does he need these qualities? He is a good performer, loves to cook, but unlike me, he likes to enjoy the process of work, not the result. When I told him that he could open his own restaurant in the future, he replied that it was too difficult and impossible. Then I doubted the need for these qualities of mine for my son.

At this stage, the question 'how' became irrelevant. I respect his choice, but he can always watch my achievement of goals and learn something for himself. We sometimes read books together about successful children who created businesses at an early age, and watch films about dreamy chefs who have achieved their goal. I even organised the Misha Cupcakes project, where he prepared cupcakes for sale when he was only 12. Despite all these actions on my part, I continue to maintain my neutrality, not trying to influence his decisions.

Of course, for some reason I was chosen as a mother to my children, and my children were chosen by me. And we should get something important as a result of the exchange of our values, but we must always respect the boundaries of each other. Sometimes, in the desire to bring good to the child, we put pressure on him, demanding to adopt a certain format of thinking. Therefore, I still suggest that before you give him what seems obvious and necessary to you, ask the above three key questions: "Why? What? How?"

We should pass on our values generously, but in no way coercively.

Questions and practice:

1. What did your parents teach you? What values did they give you while bringing up?
2. What would you like to convey to your children, what to teach?
3. Try this method with questions: "Why? What? How?" (if you already have children) and think about the answers.
4. Speak to your parents about their desire to convey certain values to you. Share your thoughts about it and start living your own life. The same conversation is better to do with your children (if you have children already?) Let them say what values they want to get from you and why.

17

Hint Signs in the Process of Finding a Destination. Importance of Accepting the Offers

"A coincidence will always be a coincidence until its significance is realised."
– Angie Corbett-Kuiper

I distinctly remember my first training in my life. It was a thick line separating me into two stages of self-perception: 'Katya is not okay' and 'Katya is full of potential and opportunities'. It was a training 'Transfer of reality'. At that time, its cost was significantly high for me. I had to give away almost a month of my earnings. But later I didn't regret it, as it changed my life radically. But more on that later.

Now I want to share with you the valuable and significant that I received from the training, which is also a necessary knowledge and way in search of our purpose. I will call it: 'Dialogue with God (Universe)'. After the first day of training, we were given homework to observe the signs. Every day and every moment God speaks to us (I will say God, but you can choose in what you believe). He communicates with us in signs. And we can see these signs everywhere. I remember I went outside after the first day of my training and for the first time began to look around in search of signs. At first it seemed to me that it was some kind of stupidity where I would find these signs. Suddenly, before my eyes, I saw a large signboard, and there it was written: 'Search and you will find what you need!'

Goosebumps ran through my body. Then I continued to look for other signs. They did not keep me waiting, they appeared like stars in the evening sky: 'You can!', 'Are you ready?', 'Your stop', 'Who are you?', 'Nothing is impossible'. And even when crossing the road, the green light was always on for me.

Since then, I have been living in a fairy tale where God speaks to me at every step.

It is such a wonderful insight that you are not alone, that you are constantly being helped and given directions on your life path, given clues and signals. These signs surround us all the time, you just need to start observing around: look at the surrounding space, listen to the words and sounds, feel the signals in your body and soul. This divine dialogue never leaves us for a moment. We are constantly under the watchful eye of the sky. The sky needs to help us because we are the executors of his light on earth. The higher your mission, the stronger you will be signalled and prompted.

After that incident-awakening, I began to see the signs constantly. I could no longer read books without looking for the answer line for myself. I watched a movie and suddenly heard a clear phrase, as if it was addressed only to me. I spoke with people and unpacked the signs in their answers. I often asked questions to the soul and turned on the observation mode. I didn't just believe that a sign would now appear to me, I knew that it would definitely come to me, that there was no doubt about it.

It happens that you receive an important answer for you at the most boring event or conversation. Here the sign is already given through your inner feeling. I remember going to a lecture on business, it was so boring and uninteresting that I didn't notice how I dozed off. When I opened my eyes, it was like lightning struck my subconscious. I knew where to go and what to do. After the lecture, I went out into the street and a smile of awareness and happiness shone on my face.

People often do not believe that they are trying to help through different channels, they want to think that they themselves can deal with everything and that they can rely only on themselves. However, we can remain strong and persistent in our aspirations, and test our assumptions through the signs around us, peering and listening to the Universe.

If you're asking questions to the sky or asking for help, you should know the answers are already for you and will soon be beaconing you everywhere. Try to turn on awareness, catch them, and of course, take them into account when you make decisions.

It happens that you ask for help, and the sky immediately reacts and sends you a person or an event, but you don't go to take it, miss an important dialogue or event where, according to the scenario of heaven, you should get a hint. It seems to you that now is not the time and place for such meetings and events. Namely, through them you could realise a lot for yourself and get what you want.

Let me give you an example of how one of my clients wanted to open her own music school. She wrote a business plan, looked for a room, but all the time something stopped her, there was fear and indecision, she lacked the necessary impetus for action. Every evening she reflected on her dream project. And when she was invited to different meetings or events, she usually refused, referring to the fact that there was no mood and strength. And the sky insistently invited her to leave the house and receive a vital message. Once, she nevertheless accepted an invitation to a charity evening. She reluctantly agreed, confident that she would sit there without any mood all evening. When she arrived, she was seated next to a man who smiled politely at her and greeted her. They started talking. It turned out that this man is a saxophonist, he has his own music school and he is very professional in the topic that worried my client. She felt determined to share her plans with him. When she revealed all her business ideas and dreams, suddenly he offered her cooperation, offering her his help. He was going to leave the country, and his students remained in the city, so he can give her his student base already. It seemed to her some incredible fairy tale. Her dream was so close. She just had to go to a charity event and get to know this man. She might have thought it was just a coincidence, or she might have believed that she needed to get out of her comfort zone and go out into the world to get her answers. Help came to her where it was called.

When people offer you some help or invite you somewhere, offer something, advise something, do not refuse immediately, but try to listen to your intuition, ask your soul whether it is worth going and accepting the offer. If you hear the answer: "Yes," then feel free to get up and go, even if you have no strength and energy, if you are not in the mood and you want to lock yourself at home and cry. You should know how to accept help from heaven, as it tries to reach you in different ways.

I like one anecdote that just reveals the above theory of help.

There was a severe flood in the city. One man sat on the roof of his house and prayed for salvation. A boat of rescuers swam up to him, and they offered him to get into the boat.

"Oh no," came the reply. "I believe that God will save me."

Soon the man heard the rumble of a helicopter above him. A ladder was lowered down to him and offered to climb up.

"No," the man shouted, "God will save me!"

Soon the water covered the roof and the man drowned. When he appeared before God, he asked: "How is it that I believed, God, that you would save me, but you didn't save me?"

God answered him: "I sent a boat for you, you did not want to be saved. Then I sent a helicopter, you again refused, why are you still indignant?"

In our destiny, a lot of useful things for the world are sealed, therefore, we and our requests are treated with due respect, sending tips and help through various channels, sending us people or circumstances.

Start today to observe around you, read signs-messages, read books and write out phrases that resonate with you, watch films or theatre performances and note what has fallen on your soul, ask the body and watch its reaction, listen to the words of people and check their messages with your soul.

LOOK! LISTEN! FEEL! REALISE!

Questions and practice:

1. Be attentive the whole day and notice the signs everywhere (billboards, notice boards, road signs, words from the books, articles etc.) Write

down them and analyse what they mean for you. Try implementing this habit in your life.

2. Always say: "Yes." Do you remember this funny approach from the comedies? But I suggest playing this game for a minimum of one day. Accept invitations and go to get the answers from the sky.

3. Remember the moments from your biography when certain meetings or situations influenced your life dramatically. What life would you have now, if this meeting or situation hadn't happened?

18
How Important is Education for the Realisation of Destiny

"The only person who is educated is the one who has learned how to learn…and change."

– Carl Rogers

A certain practice of obtaining a profession has been formed in the world. First you need to study at school, then immediately enter a higher educational institution, and only after that look for your job. Only a few violate this system, find their sense earlier and try to realise themselves in some kind of business they like. But they are haunted by sidelong glances and condemnation that they allegedly act in a wrong way. Everything must be done step by step!

In the modern world, there are now two camps of people: supporters of the academic approach and those who believe that they do not need a higher education for work. My position will not fully coincide with either of these camps.

But first I want to analyse each of them.

What are the disadvantages of strict implementation of the phased education:

1. Students are constantly learning, but do not try themselves in the business. They do not understand WHY they need this knowledge. They take theory exams without understanding or feeling how it can be useful to them in the realisation of their mission, in their work. This over time threatens with the fact that they lose interest in the profession.

2. Our education comes down most often to motivate students – to pass exams, get a diploma, or, as it is now fashionable to call it, get a 'paper'. However, after graduating from higher educational institutions, they feel lost with their medals and honours.

3. After finishing school, children often do not know at all what they want to become. But parents are afraid of condemnation from their environment, and they send their children to study for prestigious professions, or if there is little money, at least somewhere, if only they get some education. In some countries, children can get a Gap year, when they can look for themselves during the year: travel, work as volunteers, try their hand at different things, or at least just take a break from the heavy load of the school curriculum.

4. Time is lost during training. Many people may argue with me, but I do not like to waste a day of my life on useless things. I started working when I was still a schoolgirl. Throughout my academic journey, I have steadily continued to teach and fulfil my purpose. Education didn't hinder me much, but it didn't help much either. I believe that the older we get, the more knowledge about mental tasks we forget. Therefore, the sooner we begin to reveal ourselves, the better it will be.

This list is far from exhaustive. A separate book could be written on this subject. Here I just showed that everything is not as perfect as we suppose. This educational system was created by people. We are free individuals and can always change our system of worldview, study where we want and when we want. Going to high school immediately after secondary school, so that it would be good for everyone, will not definitely lead a person to success.

Regarding those people who are completely against education, I can also highlight my own special observance.

If a person tries his hand in business, if he realises that this is exactly what he wants to do in life and it will give him the opportunity to realise his purpose, then he needs to get a certain fundamental knowledge base, a support on which he will rely on. If it is possible to get it without a higher institution, then he can take training, courses, read books and start working. But not all professions allow such a luxury. Often, you need to get deep knowledge in a certain area. For example, doctors, engineers, scientists and so on.

So, as it can be seen from all of the above, any approach has its own characteristics, and each person chooses only the path that suits him the most. If he needs to get a knowledge base at the university, then he will go to study. If he can realise himself without studying at a higher educational institution or even without obtaining special certificates, he is free to work in this way as well.

It is important for me to convey the idea that you should not treat all people equally and that everyone should go through the same career stages. We are all different and our ways of achieving goals are also different. Someone can still invent something unique as a schoolboy, get a patent and develop his theme of invention all his life.

The main task of parents is to give the child an awareness of what his inclinations and abilities are, in which he can succeed in life. And let him decide himself where he should move and whether he should study further or build a career already. There are no clear rules for success, everything is always individual.

Questions and practice:

1. What special skills do you need for realising your purpose?
2. Where and how can you obtain appropriate knowledge?
3. Think about different ways to get certain knowledge and practice for achieving your goal. And choose the easiest and the most effective for you.

4. Read a biography book about the person who inspires you and find out about his/her way to success. What education do/did they have?

5. Can you realise your purpose of life now and start doing practice? Do you have enough resources? Why don't you start? What are you afraid of?

19
Your Purpose of Life should not Depend on Pride and Ego

**"Manifest plainness,
Embrace simplicity,
Reduce selfishness,
Have few desires."**

— Lao Tzu

A person, when he goes to his destination, can fall into the trap of his own ego. When he is good at what he is capable and talented in, then he wants to be more significant and important, and the opinion of others becomes extremely valuable for him, he seeks approval in the society that surrounds him. And in this constant desire to be noticed, approved, praised, he loses the sincerity of the realisation of his purpose.

On the satisfaction of self-importance, the vast majority of our energy is spent. This is especially evident in our constant concern about how we will be perceived, how we present ourselves, what impression we make. We are always extremely worried about whether others will like us, whether we are recognised and admired. If we were able to get rid of the feeling of self-importance even partially, two extraordinary things would happen to us. First, the energy that feeds our illusion of our own greatness would be released. Secondly, there would be enough free energy to penetrate into the sphere, which would allow us to be more dedicated to our purpose and be in harmony with the Universe.

It is considered to be a delusion that when we find our purpose, we will definitely be successful and wealthy in society. This may upset you, but this is not an obligatory element of the meaning of life. Not all gurus, sages and people who really realise their purpose on Earth were successful and famous. I say even more, there were those who were very poor. But they always had harmony in their hearts, and they fulfilled their life tasks from day to day. They did not seek praise for their merit, they simply did what they had to.

When a person thinks that having found the meaning of life, he will be above the rest, then this is already wrong, not the road that will lead to the truth. Destiny is not always a gift wrapped in a bright package, it is also a certain responsibility and spiritual obligation.

Of course, many happy people who know their meaning in life and find their purpose are in abundance. However, one must be extremely attentive to the thoughts, not considering oneself better than others, not being superior over other people, not depending on enthusiastic speeches addressed to oneself and praise. To know that what you have been given is a gift worth sharing with the world, and not something you have just acquired and something you have personally excelled at.

The key signs that we are all in our place and fulfilling our purpose are the cases when people come to us and thank us for the positive impact on their lives. It's like a signal that we're doing the right thing. However, you should not forget when, receiving such gratitude every day, you feel that you are almost a god in what you give to people. The main thing here is to find the golden meaning, to remember that you are just a transmitter who is realising your life purpose. It is easy to give away your sense without thinking about your perfection. Keep doing what you like but be attentive in order not to be caught into the trap of ego.

Questions and practice:

1. Have you ever had such egoistic thoughts and considered yourself as a saver for someone?
2. Find out information about great personalities who were not very successful and rich but made a great influence on history.
3. Are you afraid of people's opinion while achieving your purpose?

20
Why Were We Born the People Who We Are

"If you can accept the indescribable nature of your true identity, you unveil the mystery of life."

– Akemi G, Why We Are Born: Remembering Our Purpose through the Akashic Records

The world is woven from a billion sparks of souls, and the biggest part of it is our souls, humans', the necessary links of the entire Earth system. Remove at least one small link and the whole world's harmony can be shaken.

A person is born to perform a certain task, it can be inscribed in his destiny, or it can exist apart. In any case, his actions affect someone's life in some way. It directly or immediately concerns all mankind.

We are all catalysts for change, we are all important components of the formula for world happiness. There is nothing superfluous or unnecessary in us in the realisation of our purpose. We are assembled by the soul from the right bricks.

During our life, we may not like something in us, we find flaws and shortcomings in character, appearance and other qualities. But it is they who determine our personality, expressed in our actions and decisions.

I often heard from talented people: "I'm not like everyone else and it's hard for me."

It seems to them that something is wrong with them, that they are strange and do not fit into the standards of society. They experience difficult feelings thinking that they were born in the wrong place at the wrong time. But it's not true. Their eccentricity (not strangeness), their complex inner world and sometimes atypical appearance just give them an advantage. It is this set of qualities that help them go a special way and subsequently convey to them their extraordinary vision of the world.

I want to share with you, one interesting parable that very clearly describes this trend.

Once upon a time there was a seagull. It differed from its brothers in absolutely black plumage. In its flock, it was the most vigilant and hardy bird. And then very difficult times came: frosts unprecedented for those places came. Many birds could not stand such cold weather and died.

And only a black gull dared to fly under strong gusts of icy wind and catch rare fish. Thanks to the courage of the seagull, its relatives survived. After all, it shared it with others.

The birds treated it with great respect. But still, the bird was unhappy.

"Why was I born black and lonely?"

"Why am I not like everyone else?"

"I can never be happy and have a family!" it often said to itself, sitting alone.

The seagull suffered for a long time, and finally decided to fly to distant lands, hoping to find birds similar to it. It hoped at least there to meet its chosen one. But before that, she decided to talk with the oldest and wisest seagull.

"Why do you want to fly away? After all, the flock loves you!"

"Who wants to have children from a black seagull? And I dream of having a family and becoming a mother!"

"Why do you need a family and children?" asked the old gull.

"Looking at my children, I will feel like the happiest seagull in the world. They will be very strong. And I can be proud of the fact that I gave life for them!"

"For this, you should not fly to distant countries. Anyone will be happy to become your chosen one: after all, you saved the lives of many birds. You will bring wonderful offspring that will be just as hardy. And all our next generations will become stronger and more viable," the wise bird said.

The black gull thanked her and soared into the sky. It flew swiftly over the boundless sea, and its heart overflowed with joy: "I am the chosen!"

Years have passed. The flock of black and white gulls has grown, and people began to compose legends about these amazing, strong birds. And the black gull lived a long and happy life. Only once the bird remembered her former sufferings.

It was the day when the bird told her children: "You are extraordinary!"

This parable confirms the fact that we are all unique and unrepeatable. And it's true, we are not like everyone else. We have individual characteristics that other people do not. We spin through life and dilute the world with our energy and uniqueness.

One day my daughter was playing with a friend in our yard. They played all day and she never picked up the smartphone.

In the evening, when we came home, I jokingly said to my daughter: "Anya, you see, Tanya doesn't play on the phone much like you do. Be like Tanya!"

"Do you want me to be like Tanya? Eat poorly, like Tanya, and study badly? If I were like her, I would lose my good qualities."

We laughed together and hugged.

But for me, my daughter's answer is very stuck in my memory. It turns out that when we want to be like someone else, we forget that with this example and the whole set of negative qualities of this person, we will give up our virtues.

Every person has flaws, they are necessary in order not to develop into pride. But it is important to see your strengths as well. In any way, we must see our values and share them, not hide our talents.

Why are we born like this? Because it is needed exactly in the place and at the time where we are born, because the soul knows that it is important for our evolution and that, having other qualities and appearance, we could not realise our purpose on Earth.

Questions and practice:

1. Why were you born? (answer this question objectively).
2. Draw a picture of yourself as a unique bird, animal, plant or other symbolic image. And describe it, what particular and unique features it has and why it is so precious.
3. Read the book *Jonathan Livingston Seagull* by Richard Bach.

21
How to Find Your Destination on the Dilts Pyramid?

"Flexibility comes from having multiple choices; wisdom comes from having multiple perspectives."

– Robert Dilts

There is a technique in coaching that allows us to understand at what level of development we are at the moment, what we have, what we are doing and where we are moving. When we look at our life, analyse it attentively, then we can change it for the better, and direct it to the right path of our destiny.

Climbing the levels of the Dilts pyramid, asking the right questions, we will be able to evaluate the current life, realise the reasons for our behaviour and the values that drive us, realise what inspires and what hinders our movement towards our destination.

The search for answers to vital questions is like wandering through a labyrinth with its endless intricate corridors and dead ends. Without any map or clue, finding a way out is very difficult, if not impossible. But one has only to rise to a higher level, above the labyrinth – as all the paths will be visible – all entrances and exits.

Our life is like wandering through such a maze. To understand how to find your way, you should climb a floor or two above. Only in this way it is possible to determine the best scenario for the further development of events.

To this end, it is necessary to ask the right questions at each level of the pyramid, which will encourage finding the right answers. And with each step we will rise higher and higher to the peak of our life mission, our life purpose.

The model of the technique 'Pyramid of logical levels' can be represented as follows:

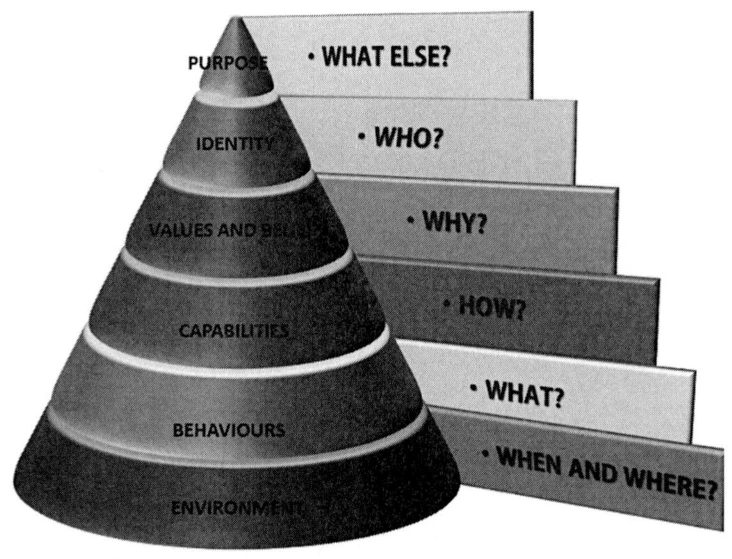

The first level answers the question: 'What do I have'.

The main question of this level is: "What do I have at the moment?" However, in order to understand the essence of this question alone, a number of additional questions should be asked:

- Am I comfortable?
- What is my environment?

- What is happening in my environment?
- Where am I or want to be?
- What place do I take in my environment, is it comfortable for me and does it correspond to what I want?
- Who is next to me, who would I like to see, and who is better to weed out from my environment?
- Someone around me helps me achieve a certain goal.

In other words, this level affects everything in all aspects of our life: material wealth, our opportunities, family, friends, place of residence. For example: where do you work, what do you do, how much do you earn, what kind of relationship do you have with your parents, do you have a family?

Try to answer these questions about your life now in order to realise what you have achieved and whether you are implementing what you wanted, to see your surroundings and analyse whether these are the people around you, whether they help your development or slow you down. To achieve your destination, you must first determine your starting point.

The second level of the pyramid asks the question: 'What am I doing'.

After analysing your current life and your surroundings, it is worth taking a look at your actions. See the chain of your daily activities that are key in building up your path of destination.

A number of important questions need to be answered, such as:

- What are you doing there to realise your purpose and your happiness?
- What do you do in life and do you like it?
- How do you conduct yourself in life?
- What are you thinking about?
- What do you get?

At this stage, you need to figure out how much what you are doing corresponds to your expectations and values. Be honest about all your routine tasks, work and family. Gather together all the activities in the circle of life balance and soberly assess their significance and importance in your life. Understand if there are any actions that are considered optional and that can be deleted from your duties. And, of course, check how your business is related to your purpose.

The third level answers the question: 'How do I choose'.

The third level of the pyramid is about your strategy. The Dilts pyramid model allows you to analyse your attitudes in detail and get to the bottom of the reasons for failures in life.

Often we dream about something, but it seems completely unrealistic and forbidden to us. But one has only to build a strategy to achieve this dream, turn it into a clear goal, then the road becomes clearer and more accessible. A person chooses his strategy for success every day: work hard towards a goal, look for other options, meet necessary people, read certain books, attend professional training and study, or be lazy, suffer, blame people around him and do anything to prove to himself that it is impossible to achieve anything in life.

When a person rises to a higher level of spirituality, then his strategy becomes simply necessary for the realisation of his destiny. His value to the world, the transfer of his gift to people become an important motivator in building a strategy and achieving the desired goal.

What is your success strategy?

What do you do every day to become who you want to be?

What are my strengths and can I rely on them to achieve the desired result?

What skills and abilities can I acquire to achieve what I want?

Can I take advantage of the abilities and opportunities of others?

The fourth level asks the question 'What do I believe in'.

This question is about our beliefs and values. At this level, we can understand what our decisions and thoughts are based on. What is the most important and valuable thing for us?

This level, in my opinion, is one of the most important in the pyramid, since it is here that the whole structure of our personality is laid. Here we realise who we really are and why we live this way and not otherwise.

Our faith and our values are what drives us and is our beacon of the soul.

The fifth level of the pyramid asks the question: 'Who am I'.

One is sure that he is a brilliant artist and designer, and therefore he can handle any exhibitions, contests, competitions and shows. Another considers himself a loser and mediocre person. Self-identification is the determining factor for success in life.

To fully realise your destiny, you need to know who you are and why you are on this Earth. When you doubt your abilities, thus identifying yourself is not obvious, erased by your fears and doubts. A person cannot be completely useful to the world if he does not see his value, if he does not declare himself to the extent that he actually has.

And the answer to the question: "Who am I" determines how he lives and how happy he is.

Look at yourself from the side, as if you were not in your body. Watch your movie of life. How would you characterise this person? He definitely deserves everything that you attributed to him and is worthy of the fact that you do not allow him.

Usually our self-identification happens subjectively with hundreds of layers of demands on ourselves and comparing ourselves with more successful and happy people.

Take a piece of paper and write honestly who you are, without comparing with anyone and without relying on anyone's opinion.

The sixth level of the pyramid asks about your mission.

This level helps to realise the importance and value of a particular person in the world. This is the peak of the pyramid, the most important part of it.

"What else am I living for?"

If you have ever asked this question, then you are already on the right track. This is the meaning of our life, this is the reason why we are on Earth.

So, now you know what the Dilts pyramid looks like and what its levels mean.

How to work with this pyramid and how can one achieve one's purpose of life by changing its certain levels?

For example:

What do I have?	I have a stable job, a small but monthly salary, my job is in my specialty, but I like to do photography in my free time. This is my hobby and I like to create beauty.
What am I doing?	I work from 8 to 7. Sometimes I work at weekends. I spend little time with my family. And there is very little time left for practice in photography.
How do I choose?	I'm afraid to quit, because this is stability, and I have to feed my family.
What do I believe?	For me, family comes first, I love them and work for them. Beauty is also important to me.
Who am I?	I am an ordinary person who lives on Earth and does his job.
Why do I live?	I live for my family.

After analysing the current life, what do you think the person who fills in this table experiences when looking at their answers?

Of course, sadness and bitterness that he cannot do what he really likes and what is important for him. However, if you change the focus and look first of all at the question: "Why do I live?" and then build the rest of the levels of life, you can thus change your life for the better. And the road to realisation will appear on the way to your destination.

Here's what a new table might look like with updated data and perceptions.

Why do I live?	To create and bring beauty and love to the world.
Who am I?	I am the one who makes this world more beautiful and happier. I am an artist, a creator.
What do I believe?	I believe that beauty makes people better, and love fills the world with light. It is important for me to convey this to people

	with my photography, my own words and actions.
How do I implement it?	First, in my free time, I take pictures for a small fee, collect a portfolio. I take courses and various kinds of photography training. I participate in competitions, exhibitions. I raise the price. Improving the camera. When my monthly income exceeds the income of my main job, I quit and do only photography.
What am I doing?	I photograph children, families, events, weddings, I earn good money.
What do I have?	My favourite hobby is my job. Surprisingly, my income from photography is much higher than my previous job. There are lots of clients and referrals. I spend more time with my family and relax more.

So, you see, it's not all that complicated. All you have to do is change your focus, and suddenly your life can be quite happy and fulfilling. We build our reality from the bricks that we choose. We are the builders of our happiness! And it depends only on us how firmly the foundation of our happy life will be laid. Now you can afford to create a life that is consistent with your purpose and your values. It's up to you! Where will you start? Fill in the plate on the Dilts pyramid from the top and move down and down until you reach the bottom and the question: "What do I have now." And now create your own 'NOW' on the basis of everything that you noted in the values and your mission. It is the only task for you after this chapter.

22
Contact with the Soul to Receive Tips on Your Destination

"I am never alone, my Soul guides me and my Guardian Angel protects me. That is teamwork at its best."

– Genevieve Gerard

I am often asked how to get answers, what training to take, or where to find such a clairvoyant or hypnotherapist who will easily and simply give us clues about our destiny. In my opinion, these are already extreme measures, which are not always reliable and honest in relation to our soul.

We have already discussed that our soul has all the necessary answers and clues. There is nothing better and more correct for us than what our soul knows. When we were babies, we lived in harmony with the soul, our reactions were spontaneous and not clouded by reason and knowledge. We were open and lighter. Now our thoughts are already filled with various arguments, reasons by the people who are trying to convince us that everything still needs to be carefully checked, redone, rethought, which is more complicated than it seems to us. We are in the chaos of our thoughts, we are completely confused about what is 'ours' and what is 'superficial, external'.

And sometimes, when we no longer have the strength to endure these voices of reproaches and restrictions, we turn to our soul, with tears, with a request to tell us how to act and where to move. But in response we get silence. Our soul would like to help us, but she no longer believes that we will fully accept its proposal and its message. It feels that we are not yet ready, that we are too overloaded with external information, our connection with the world of distractions.

In order for us to receive directly the messages of the soul, to move towards our destiny easily and naturally, we must first establish contact with it, which we have lost over many years.

How to do it?

Start by returning to your inner desires, dreams, requests, sometimes even just whims.

Every day, waking up, ask yourself what you want for yourself today. This is not pampering, not selfishness, this is a natural pattern.

Do you know what is the indicator that your contact with the soul is lost? When you are asked to write or say what you want, you will not know what to answer. It's a terrible feeling. It is similar to the state that you have completely lost yourself and your needs in life. Under no circumstances should this be allowed.

Ask questions to yourself, your soul. It may be your inner child who has been asking you for many years, for example, to skip the work day and go to the park, buy ice cream, read a book, watch an interesting movie. Sometimes your soul just needs silence and contemplation. You don't need anything, just be alone a little in this wonderful world, fill up with energy, don't rush and don't run anywhere. Be free and real.

Right now, write down on paper what you want at the moment and allow yourself to do it. Give yourself this little opportunity to touch your soul. But do not expect that it will immediately begin to reveal everything to you and share the secrets and importance. It needs more time for your channel of communication to be open.

The more you make such gifts to yourself, the more it will believe that you want to be closer to it, want to be filled with happiness, and not be in a constant race for material resources. These breaks for yourself, for the sake of your state of satisfaction and fullness will subsequently manifest itself in the fact that you will feel a surge of energy, you will better feel the world around you, your channel with your soul will open up more and more and your life will become more and more meaningful.

When you feel this fullness, when you realise that the process of awareness and understanding of yourself has begun, move on. Start sharing your energy with others, exchange what you have acquired and receive from others what they have created. You will be drawn to people: spiritual, happy, those who are ready to share themselves and their knowledge. In this energy and information exchange, you will also receive many clues to your questions about the destination. This is an incredible journey for small keys, new doors and new facets of perception.

Your soul will surely be supportive of your searches, reverent attitude towards your own requests and desires. Your soul will enjoy the fact that you care about your life, your condition, your dreams and desires to transform the world around you and, of course, your determination to realise your destiny, leaving a mark on the Earth. Finally, it will start giving you necessary clues to achieve your purpose of life. And you will get your own informator and helper who will always be in touch with you and give you directions to go.

Questions and practice:

1. Launch a daily practice, ask a question to yourself in the morning: "What do I want today for myself" and realise this wish during the day.
2. Listen carefully to your desires, tuning up to your thoughts and feeling your body. Write down these thoughts and assess them.
3. Write down a list of your wishes (from 10–50), as many as you can.

23
Finding Your Own Grail

"Your greatest self has been waiting your whole life; don't make it wait any longer."

— Steve Maraboli, Life, the Truth, and Being Free

Each person is sure that at a certain stage of life he will find what he was born for. Therefore, now everyone has rushed into psychology, esotericism, introspection and self-knowledge. They are looking for ways to understand what is allegedly closed to them, they do not know.

They are looking for something that seems to them to suddenly appear in their awareness and they will begin to live consciously in harmony with their destiny. They need the same grail that will express their value in the world and how they will differ from others.

I want to give an example of happiness. Many people live their whole lives in anticipation of happiness. Now I will suffer, but soon it will come. Here I will finish school, there is a university, they definitely say there will be more freedom and happiness. And after university, there is even more happiness, because I will be an adult and I will choose and decide everything for myself. The work is very hard now, but soon I will retire, there will definitely be more happiness. And so on… We constantly move our happiness to 'later'. But bad luck, happiness is always within us, we just need to just allow ourselves to be happy and do what we want, realise our mission now. Give yourself the opportunity to choose what we like and want right now, and not tomorrow or in a few years. Those who have known this truth, they rejoice every day, they are constantly filled with happiness, absorbing it from everywhere and receiving it from everyone they meet on their way.

The same is true with purpose. Stop looking for it outside, look for ways to achieve it. Just understand, you were born with it already. It is already included in your life package. It is an integral part of your personality, your soul. Every day, just try to live more consciously, realising that you are already giving something to the world. When we say one word to someone, this word can then fly around the world. And then back to you. This is how the law of influence waves works. We just do it all unconsciously, not seeing the point in it. But it is always there, in our life there is a lot of meaning and significance. Ask yourself what is so special about me, you are trying to make your unconscious actions understandable and increase your conscious actions. For example, you have been helping people around you for many years by giving advice on a certain topic. You can work in a completely different area, and help in another. You just like it so much, you are so drawn to it. And whether you like it or not, you are fulfilling your purpose.

A person who was able to stop, finally, see this sign, understand that his task is precisely in the actions, which he does more unconsciously, once he can take a risk and give up his job which does not fit his desire and he will follow his soul and do what he really wants.

My mother, for example, as far as I can remember, has always treated everyone as a doctor. She knows about all the medicines, all the symptoms and helps almost all members of our family. As soon as someone is ill, she is already there and treats according to her experience and knowledge. She has worked all her life at the plant as an economist, but did not dare to follow her vocation as a doctor. But despite this, she does a lot for our family, her friends, etc. She still fulfils her calling in some way. Just imagine for a moment if my mother took a chance and went to medical school and trained and became a doctor. How many more lives would she save?

So, as you can see, it's not important sometimes to look for the grail that will make us very important in the world, sometimes you just need to allow yourself to do what you are drawn to, what gives us energy and what people need. Well, if you dare and follow your calling, then you will do much more on this Earth.

Questions and practice:

1. What can you already do now which is considered to be your purpose?
2. Do you do something that you really like but do not earn money from it? How can you start earning money from this activity?
3. Draw your magic Purpose Grail and describe its features. Imagine that you have already had your own Graal and from now you can realise your life mission.

24

Do Not Focus on Your Value to the World, but Happiness

"Never regret anything that made you smile."

– Mark Twain

When we talk about purpose in life, people often associate this word with their value to the world. They present themselves as an important member of society who is useful and fulfils a significant role entrusted to him from birth. Everyone wants to be valued and needed. Partly, this is true. But at the same time, the line between value for people and the pleasure from the realisation of destiny is very fragile.

When a person finds his destiny and understands how he can manifest himself to a greater extent, then he is involved in the process of realising himself and his abilities. There are people who need his talents, his work is addictive, and his favourite hobby is already officially his vocation and life profession.

It seems that this is a logical chain and there are no particular problems in all this. However, even here depression develops over time. What was the reason?

Happiness is a balance between 'I want' and 'I need'. It's the same with purpose. When we think that we should always carry our light, share ourselves with the world, our talents, constantly concentrating on the fact that a lot depends on us and that our mission is, basically, to give, share, help, then we eventually lose our reserves of energy, our strength runs out. We forget that our soul came into this world not only for this. It also needs to enjoy life on Earth, it wants to be filled with happiness and joy during the life path. When we realise our purpose through 'I want', we do not do something opposite, we just change our focus, we change our hyper importance and hyper responsibility to the desire to do what we love, to be happy and give the world exactly as much as we are. Now we can afford it. At the same time, we are in balance, we feel harmony inside and do not go into depression and apathy.

The second important factor affecting our state is people's dependence on the constant maintenance of self-worth. The more a person raises the level of importance of his role for others, the more he reduces the level of importance of his happiness. And such a path in an effort to help people leads him in the end to misfortune and confusion. While he is valuable and people turn to him, he feels at his best, feels a surge of strength, and when he dries up, when people come to him less, it seems to him that he is not needed and not valuable. Then he asks himself the question: "What do you want now?" The answer is usually obvious. Not everyone manages to determine it. But it is simple. Everyone needs happiness, which means that by nature we strive to do only what brings us joy. It turns out that by doing what we like, getting pleasure from it, we still somehow help people, realise our destiny. In fact, we don't change anything. We do all the same important things for the world. It's just that we are distracted from our value, our meaning and importance for others, we simply share what we ourselves really like and what brings us real pleasure.

So, when you get caught in your ego trap, when you feel low and deficient in your value to the world, just ask yourself, "What do you like? What would you like to do?" And do it! Every day with enthusiasm, desire, passion and love for your work. People themselves will feel this flow and will begin to pull themselves up to your fire of happiness. They will want to bask near you, feeling your love for what you do. When your focus is on how to do what you love as soon as possible, then you will not be dependent on other people not judging you, on the number of clients or other factors that affect your confidence. You are already happy that you are implementing what is important to you. And your purpose will be simultaneously realised and your value for the world will continuously grow.

Questions and practice:

1. What is happiness to you? Write down your description of your own happiness.
2. What would you do, if you did not have to earn money?
3. What would you do if you could realise your childish dream?
4. What is your hobby? Would you be happy if you could get money from it?

25
Is it Mine Or Not?

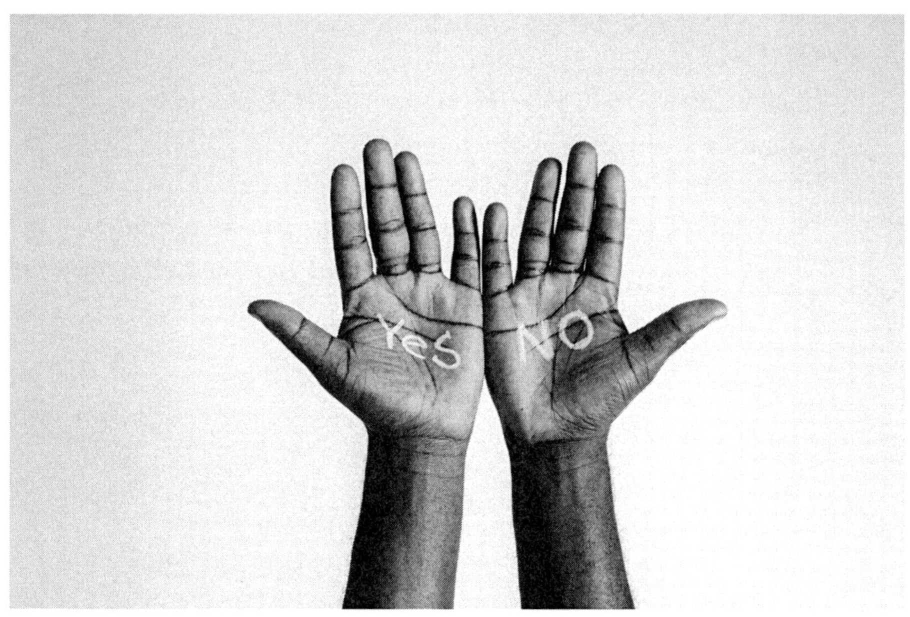

"Find out what you like doing best and get someone to pay you for doing it."
– Katherine Whitehorn

Often people ask the question: "What I do is mine?" They recall how they started their career, trying to figure out if it was their intention or they chose under the influence of external factors. And the answer is: "EVERYTHING in the world is YOURS!" Just take it and try it! The world is full of opportunities and chances to test yourself and your abilities. Can you say for sure that you have tried all your natural gifts that God has placed in you? I think no.

People often do not understand that there are no limits to our capabilities. Once on Earth, we are given at the same time the entire earthly field to practice our skills. Our talents cannot disappear or change, only our needs change during a certain period of our growing up.

Remember your childhood, when you were little and wanted to try everything, to figure everything out. You were forbidden, but you still tried and got it. You thus revealed your purpose, you were not afraid, you did not reflect on the topic: 'Yours or not yours'. You were just interested, you enjoyed the process. If you painted, you painted without thinking how beautiful it was. You just wanted to draw. If you sang, you sang with an open heart. If you made something, then it was exciting for you to see the result. Now, if we, adults, could take this lightness and non-judgmentalness of children and apply it in life. And then such verification questions disappear. We will just allow ourselves to do what we want to do, go where we want to go and be ourselves.

Our light and our life values are always with us. Wherever we go, they never leave us. Our destiny is beside us. The main thing is that in the soul it is peace and happiness. We do not torture ourselves with questions about how to choose what is ours and what we are good at. When this focus of attention and analysis disappears, then the movement through life becomes freer, actions are more courageous, and there is more joy and happiness in the soul. Isn't that the most important thing in life?

Sometimes it seems to me that I still have so many unknown and interesting things inside me to discover and share, and I still want to try more and more. I simply allow myself this freedom and do not choose what is mine or what is not mine. And there is so much more to discover and so much more to share! Apparently, I do not stop in any way and improve my life every time. While someone decides 'Mine or not mine', I act and get success.

Questions and practice:

1. What did you use to do in childhood and get excited about?
2. What other spheres are interesting for you? Write a list (even if you do not have any qualification or experience).
3. Imagine that you are in a shop with a variety of jobs and you could get any one from any shelf, what would you ask and why?

26
Final Motivational Words

Be brave and take your first step towards your realisation of your purpose of life.

Be strong and persistent and follow your dream until you fulfil it.

Be patient while you are reaching your goals.

Be yourself and open for new opportunities and chances.

Value your life and everything that you possess and people who love you.

Take care of your soul's wishes and do what it needs.

Realise yourself, your purpóse of life, your talents and skills. Be generous in sharing your gifts.

Believe that you are unique and your values are significant for this world and realisation of your purpose of life is a vital door for someone.

It is time to open this door and declare who you are!

You can definitely do it! And certainly BE happy!

A road to the purpose of life is endlessly long, so it is high time to take a first step towards it.

Go!

I believe

in you!

27

Coach Questions of Purpose of Life

1. What directions do you see as possible?
2. What will you convey in any profession?
3. What in life do you do differently than other people?
4. How will you differ from other professionals?
5. What are you most proud of in your current life? Why does this make you happy?
6. What in my current life am I most grateful for? Why does this make me happy?
7. What will you bring to any field of activity?
8. What is your uniqueness?
9. How do I inspire people?
10. What ideas inspire you the most?
11. What environment would you like to have?
12. What things do you like doing over and over again?
13. What life events make you talk about them with excitement?
14. What have you always wanted to share with others?
15. What accomplishments would you like to share with others?
16. What do you have that other people don't have?
17. What do you like to talk about the most?
18. What makes you smile?
19. Who is your biggest inspiration?
20. What are you especially good at?
21. If you had to teach someone something, what would you teach?
22. What would you like to pass on to your next generations?
23. What advice do people usually turn to you for? On what topic?
24. What do people admire about you or what do they love about you?

25. What are some of your strengths that someone who loves you would highlight?

26. What could you train in for a long time?

27. What in your life would you like to make more time for?

28. What do you not get tired of?

29. What did you want to do, but never did, what stopped you?

30. What could you do differently knowing that no one will judge you?

31. When was the last time you began to act, having only the germ of an idea in your head, but at the same time already strong belief in it?

32. Remember what you were doing so enthusiastically that you forgot to eat or go to the toilet?

33. If you had to perform in front of a lot of people, what would your performance be about? Who would these people be?

34. When and under what circumstances have I felt most alive lately?

Powerful Questions

35. What would you do even if you were severely punished for it?

36. What matters to you?

37. What skills of mine could I mix together so that the result is interesting to other people?

38. If you were given the opportunity to tell a little: 'About yourself', but only in two sentences, what would they be?

39. If you could send a message to the whole world, what would you say in 30 seconds?

40. If you could live the same day over and over again, what would you rather do on that day?

41. What will you regret that you didn't do in your life?

42. How would the world have changed if you had not been born?

43. If you were allowed to change one thing in the world. What was that?

44. What can inspire you so much that you wake up in the morning with the words: "Hurrah! A new day begins!"

45. What would you take a bullet for? What important goal is worth living so much that you can let it become more important than your life?

46. Imagine that you have all the material goods of the world, and you never have to work again, you have so much money that you cannot spend everything. What would you dedicate your life to?

47. And if you were very poor or if you were in a place where your main activity is impossible, what would you do?

48. If you knew you had a year to live, what would you do?

49. What would you like to be written about in an obituary?

50. What would you do if you were 100 % sure you couldn't fail?

51. If you had only one wish, what would it be?

52. What kind of person would you like to live?

53. What would you like to change in this world?

54. What would you like to accomplish before leaving this world?

55. What would you like to hear about yourself at the funeral?

56. What would you most like to be recognised for in your life?

57. How will I live in 5, 10, 15 years without realising my destiny?

58. Imagine that you are already 90 years old. You are sitting in a rocking chair on the porch of your house and basking in the gentle rays of spring. You are happy and relaxed, you are satisfied with the wonderful life that has been given to you. You remember your whole life, think about what you achieved during this life and what you had. What would you think of first?

59. How do I want to be remembered in this life?

60. If you could get a tattoo, what was it about, what did it mean and what power did it give?

61. If your soul could now say words that are important to you, what would it say?